KU-097-065

FOSSILS
A Study in Evolution

J. O. I. Spoczynska
FRES FZS FBIS

With line drawings by Melchior Spoczynski

FREDERICK MULLER

First published in Great Britain in 1971 by
Frederick Muller Limited, 110 Fleet Street, London E.C.4

Copyright © J. O. I. Spoczynska, 1971

All rights reserved. No part of this publication may be
reproduced, stored in a retrieval system, or transmitted,
in any form or by any means, electronic, mechanical,
photocopying, recording or otherwise, without the prior
permission of Frederick Muller Limited.

Printed in Great Britain by The Anchor Press Ltd.,
and bound by William Brendon & Son Ltd.,
both of Tiptree, Essex

SBN: 584 10093 0

C. F. MOTT COLLEGE OF EDUCATION

75635

FOSSILS
A Study in Evolution

Contents

Illustrations

Plates

Acknowledgement

The photographic plates in this book are reproduced by
courtesy of the American Museum of Natural History

This book
is gratefully dedicated to
the memory of
J. L. B. SMITH

Introduction

W HY study fossils?

The romance of the earth has always fascinated and intrigued mankind. Long before the dawn of Christianity the Greek historians were expounding their theories, some fanciful, others with a remarkable degree of insight. In the writings of Aristotle one finds references to 'creatures from another world' which had reached this planet and whose remains had been buried in the rocks. Aristotle was wrong in thinking that they had dropped from outer space; but he did not fail to recognise the fact that they were indeed relics of living things which had, in some way, become imprisoned in the rocks.

The story of the earth is the most fascinating of all volumes. It is an open book which all may read if only they will take the trouble to understand the significance of the various phenomena exhibited in the different strata, just as the would-be reader of the printed book must first familiarise himself with its symbols, in this case the alphabet. It is not really so much more difficult to become a student of palaeontology—a word which means 'knowledge of ancient life'— than it is to learn a language or to study the classics; but the book of the rocks is inscribed, not in words, but with clearly-defined and recognisable forms, and the story of the earth divides naturally into equally clearly-defined chapters: in other, words the successive periods of geological time. A comparative time-scale will be found on page 184.

Certain fossils are found only in particular strata, and these latter are composed only of certain specific types of rock. These characteristic fossils are called 'indicator fossils' and, as this term implies, they act as pointers to a particular period of geological time. It will be seen from this that if fossils A and B are found only in beds of, say, Carboniferous age, should they turn up in combination with Permian rocks, which date from a much later period, one must draw the conclusion that movements of the earth's crust have thrown these earlier beds up. The intrusion of Carboniferous fossils A and B among C and D which are found only in Permian strata is, therefore, a definite indication of earth movement at some time or another. On this basis one can make certain deductions; for example, if A and B are found mixed with C and D at *several different places* on the earth's surface, the same type of volcanic activity or other earth movement must have been responsible in all cases, probably, though not necessarily, at the same time. If C and D only are found in Permian beds, this presupposes that the earlier Carboniferous beds containing A and B will be found underlying the Permian strata, as would normally occur if no cataclysmic events had taken place. It is problems like these that make the study of fossils so interesting.

One of the most important aspects of palaeontology—perhaps *the* most important—is the way in which the fossil record lays out before us, as it were, a map showing the evolution of all life on earth, up to and including mankind. From the simplest unicellular organism to the most highly-developed forms of life a pattern can be seen emerging at all points: even in the most widely-divergent branches of evolution this same pattern can be observed, linking totally unrelated forms. This parallel evolutionary pattern is seen at its most striking when comparing the fossils from the Old and the New Worlds, and continues to be apparent in the living forms representing the same major groups in the Americas on the one hand and Asia and Africa on the other. Australia, again, is in a unique position, in that relic forms have been isolated on what is, in effect, a large island; the lack of contact with the mainland of the larger continents has produced tendencies towards specialisation which have not been paralleled elsewhere.

The fossil fishes represent, from many viewpoints, the most important of all the prehistoric forms of life which the fossil record has revealed. Evolutionarily speaking, the fishes form the most direct link between the origin of life in the water and its eventual emergence on to the land, which gave rise ultimately to mammals, primates and man. This can be proved in a good many ways, all of which will be dealt with in due course; but before one can trace this progress from the earliest life in the water to the colonisation and eventual domination of the land by forms specifically adapted to exploit the possibilities opened up by this new way of life, one must be able to recognise the forms themselves and their origins, and the rocks which are typical of the specific strata in which these forms occur.

A number of fossil groups are not discussed here because, in spite of their general importance, they have no bearing on the descent of man from the vertebrate stem. An example is the Mollusca. When the basic principles of palaeontology have been mastered, we can turn to tracing the story of the development of life from its simplest beginnings to its widest implications in the present-day life on this planet. Since the Devonian era was the great turning-point when the ancestry of man was first laid down, we shall turn more of our attention to this particular period. The Devonian era has aptly been called 'the Age of Fishes', and it is in the rocks of this period that most of the most fascinating secrets of our own existence lie buried.

I

The Book of the Rocks

I N A printed book such as this one the various aspects of the main theme are split up into chapters; this not only helps the reader to simplify his approach to the subject, but also serves to show a relationship between the various aspects concerned. This same analogy can be applied to the study of earth history. Much in the same way as political history is divided into periods, all naturally falling into a recognisable and clearly-defined pattern, the history of the earth is in similar fashion clearly sub-divided into a number of aspects, or chapters, all of which have a certain interrelationship and whose sub-division in this way simplifies the task of the student approaching the study of earth history for the first time.

The rocks which form the Earth's crust are of three main types: the original or first rocks, formed by the cooling of lava after the eruption of volcanoes and from molten rock thrust upwards into the crust from the earth's interior. These rocks are known as *igneous rocks*—rocks 'formed by fire'; such rocks cannot, of course, contain fossils. They are the oldest of all rocks, and form a substratum for subsequent earth activities such as land subsidences, the encroachment of the waters and the building of mountain chains.

Rocks of the second type are known as *sedimentary rocks*, which, as their name implies, are formed by the deposition of layers of earth, sand, silt and other materials eroded from pre-existing rocks and carried by rivers or by other means to the oceans or to the inland lakes, and are there compressed into layers. These comprise the majority of all rocks, and contain almost all known fossils.

Finally we have the *metamorphic rocks*, which are the result of physical and chemical changes when igneous or sedimentary rocks (or both) are affected by cataclysmic events, such as the rise of molten magma from the core of the Earth, deep burial, applied stress, glaciation and other extreme phenomena which affect them to such an extent that their basic nature is altered beyond recognition. Any fossils originally present in sedimentary strata which have been changed into metamorphic rocks by violent processes of this kind are in most cases destroyed, and it is therefore of little use looking for fossils in metamorphic rocks.

The great majority of rocks are of sedimentary origin, the most well-known ones being limestone, sandstone, oolites, chalk, shale, mudstone and clay. All the above can be sub-divided into various formations, which again are characterised by specific features which are very typical and absent from other formations. Apart from this, great numbers of fossils are typically found only in certain well-defined strata; for example, certain fossils of the Upper Lias deposits will not be found in the Lower Lias; and so on.

This particular fact is not really so very strange when you come to think about it, because, after all, the animals and plants now living on Earth are subject to pretty much the same type of restrictions. Animals and plants of the tropical jungle will not grow in our temperate climate; the flora and fauna of the Arctic Circle would find tropical temperatures insupportable. This, of course, is a very wide and sweeping generalisation, but within this framework are finer distinctions which hold good just as inexorably. For example, in the tropics we have dry, arid regions at one end of the scale, wet monsoon lands at the other, and a variety of temperature and humidity variation ranges in the middle. The plants and animals in all of these regions are entirely different; there is very little over-lapping.

Coming down to an even finer scale of distinction, let us look at the inhabitants of Britain which, being a small island compared with the rest of the world, can be said to have a reasonably stable climate, with, of course, slight local variations due to altitude and proximity to the sea.

Let us look at the flora and fauna of woodlands for our first example. Even these will vary according to whether the woodlands are coniferous or deciduous. If the latter, the species of animals and plants will to a great extent depend on the type of soil underlying the particular woodland in question: in other words, the type of rock in that particular part of the country. The plants of chalk soils, which are known as *calcicoles*, will not be found growing on an acid, peaty soil or on a heavy clay; conversely, the plants of these regions cannot abide calcareous soils and are, therefore, known as *calcifuges*.

Animals, of course, are in the first instance dependent on the plant life, and the type of animal which inhabits the flora of chalk soils will be absent from plant communities growing on soils of a different type. As a very well-known example of this, the swallow-tail butterfly is restricted entirely to one or two small localities in the Norfolk Broads where the foodplant of the larva, hog's fennel *(Peucedanum palustre)* grows. The caterpillar feeds only on this plant, which will thrive only in a very acid peaty or boggy type of habitat.

To carry this analysis a stage further, certain birds will nest only in certain types of trees. The occurrence of these trees is dictated by the type of woodland, which is again dependent on the structure of the underlying rock. Clay retains water, while sand and gravels provide excellent drainage; here we have the makings of a very obvious distinction between wet and dry woodland.

In the woodland itself, of whatever type, we have the floor layer, the herb layer and the shrub layer, and lastly the upper regions among the leaves and branches of the trees themselves, from the lower branches to the canopy. All these microhabitats support entirely different animal populations. The small insects and worms which live in the soil will not be found at the tops of the trees; the ground-nesting birds will not build in the branches. Caterpillars which eat the foliage of the trees will not be found living on the plants which grow beneath the shade of the boughs.

Moving now away from the woodlands, we find an entirely new series of populations in coastal areas. Salt marshes and mud-flats will support life of an entirely different type from that characteristic of sand-dunes and marram-grass. Exposed stretches of coast such as those found at the tops of cliffs and on ledges facing the wind offer very different living conditions, and animals and plants occupying these niches will need to have special adaptations for their survival such as, for example, the xerophytic modifications found in the leaves of plants which must conserve moisture in order to survive at all. Animals which are exposed to salt spray, if not themselves semi-aquatic, must have some built-in biological protection against an excess of sodium chloride in the body. All these things tend to separate populations into sharply-defined colonies with very little, if any, overlapping; nowhere is this more apparent than in plant successions, such as can be seen when fenland fills up and is overtaken by carr and sedge, finally reverting to scrub, heath and woodland.

It should now be easy to see why certain types of fossils are so characteristic of specific strata. The strata represent the particular living conditions that were in existence at the time that these plants or animals were living, and they could not have existed in any different type of habitat. It is not, of course, always known precisely what the habitat in question was like, though a good deal of knowledge may be gained through deductions made from the types of fossils themselves. Marine shells, for example, would not be found in the coal forests, nor would small birds' remains be found in strata where no insect life had occurred.

The food chain is one of the most important aspects of the whole of the life-pattern, as without food of one kind or another no life could exist. When, therefore, it is known that a particular animal whose fossil remains occurred in a certain rock fed on some particular other animal, then naturally the fossils of both would tend to occur in the same strata, but those of the predator would be more numerous than those of the prey.

This now brings us to a rather interesting point. In some rocks it has been found that where a predator-prey relationship had been established in some particular formation, later strata exhibited decreasing numbers of the predators and a corresponding increase in the numbers of the prey. The most likely explanation for this would seem to be that climatic changes had made the habitat unsuitable for the predator, which gradually became extinct, but that the prey was able, in some way, to adapt itself to changing conditions and eventually supersede the predator numerically. If the process had been reversed and the changing habitat had proved unsuitable for the prey, then the predator, too, would have become extinct owing to the fact that its food supply would have died out. Though this phenomenon can, of course, occur, it would appear to be less common than the reverse. The fossil record thus becomes a pointer: if one type of organism flourishes at the expense of another, this will perhaps indicate a climatic change of moderate severity, while if both organisms appear to have become extinct more or less simultaneously, a more violent change of climate is indicated.

The plant life of the remote past was, as it is today, governed by interrelated factors in which geographical location, the prevalence or otherwise of winds, the degree of humidity, the temperature range and the type of soil all played their part. It is also fairly safe to assume that a good many of these specific sets of conditions then existing have no counterpart in the world today, or only to a very limited extent.

A case in point is the great carboniferous forests which make up the Coal Measures. The typical trees of the Coal Measures were cycads, cordaites, scale-trees, giant horsetails and the like, which are either extinct or practically so to-day. Huge forests of ginkgo trees extended for thousands of miles, some of them 200 ft. high, in Carboniferous times; the only living representative of this family to-day is the maidenhair tree *(Ginkgo biloba)*, which is found growing wild only in one or two isolated parts of Japan and elsewhere, but which may be seen growing in cultivation in gardens, both public and private, in various parts of Britain, especially in the more southerly areas. The scale trees *(Lepidodendron)*, giants of the past, are dwarfed into insignificance by their tiny present-day representative, *Selaginella*, which is about three or four inches high, although common enough in damp places. The common horsetail *(Equisetum vulgare)*, which grows on damp river banks and near ponds, never grows more than a few inches in height, but the horsetails of the Carboniferous forests were about 160 feet in height. It can hardly be disputed that the main reason for this vast difference is purely and simply that the particular combinations of habitat factors requisite for the growth of the coal forests simply do not exist to-day.

2

The Earliest Fossils

SCIENTISTS have calculated the age of the oldest rocks to be some-where in the region of 3800 million years, the actual formation of the Earth having probably occurred about one million years before this. Even with modern methods such as the use of isotopes and the measurement of radiation, it is still not possible to calculate the exact length of time in precise figures; but for our purposes the above estimate will suffice.

Life could not develop while the Earth's surface was still seething with molten magma; but, much later, when this had cooled to form our earliest igneous rocks, life at its very simplest and most primitive level of organisation began to stir in the warm primeval waters. Chemical and atmospheric gases helped to create proteins and amino-acids from jelly-like protoplasmic substances which had the power of growth. These substances developed mobile properties, enabling them to cover greater areas, and their method of reproduc-tion was probably amoeboid. By means of binary fission microscopic specks of matter—the forerunners of the cell—were able to multiply and absorb oxygen from the water to combine with the various chemical properties of the protoplasmic matter itself.

The above is more or less a conjecture as to the origin of life on Earth, since obviously there can be no fossil records left by soft substances. Only those later forms which were able to secrete hard calcareous or siliceous shells around their soft parts could leave behind them any traces of their existence.

Before animal life could exist, plant life had to appear. Plants are able to manufacture their own food by the action of sunlight on their green colouring matter, or chlorophyll, in the process called photo-synthesis. The animals which form the lowest link in the food chain subsist on plants, and animals higher in the food chain may feed upon the animals which are dependent on the plants. In this way even carnivorous animals are ultimately dependent on plants, as

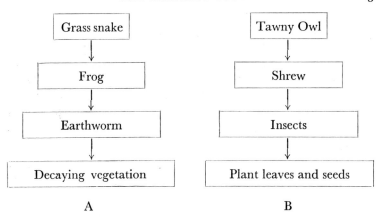

A

B

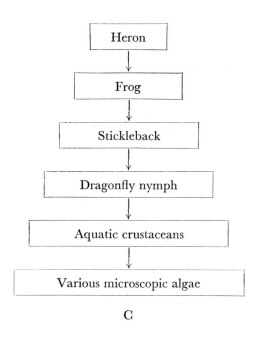

C

FIG 1   Some typical food chains: (a) and (b) in a wood, (c) in a freshwater pond

may be seen from a glance at some typical food chains (Fig. 1). This is one of the basic fundamentals of biology.

The query now arises: how did the first plants come into existence? In other words, how did they start to manufacture chlorophyll to develop the nutritional processes of photosynthesis, and thus differentiate themselves from what we will now refer to as 'animals' —in other words, living things devoid of chlorophyll? It is difficult to say with any certainty how this came about, but the most likely explanation is that this occurred when masses of protoplasm floated on or just below the surface of the waters, where the temperature and other conditions were very different from those obtaining in the depths. The action of sunlight itself may have caused certain chemical changes in the protoplasm which, in turn, may have given rise to nuclear changes causing the formation of chlorophyll. This might well have, in its turn, responded to the further action of sunlight by giving rise to a series of chemical changes in which the newly-formed chlorophyll acted as a catalyst, itself remaining unchanged while enabling the organism to form carbohydrates and other nutritive substances. The repeated continuation of these processes eventually led to some differentiation of cell activities, whereby some parts of the organism were specifically adapted to nutritional functions, while others remained unaffected and carried on the processes of growth and reproduction.

In time, masses of these newly-formed microscopic plants died and sank to the bottom. The amoeba-like microscopic organisms which abounded on the soft mud or sand of the ocean bed engulfed these chlorophyll-bearing organisms, and were able to expand their life processes by increasing their chemical scope, as it were, through the ingestion of nitrogen and other chlorophyll-activated substances. The chlorophyll itself did not become part of their tissues, but retained its essential function of a catalytic agent; the nitrogen, carbohydrates and other substances which are the end-products of chlorophyll were absorbed into the body of non-photosynthetic organisms. In this way a higher degree of specialisation was enabled to be brought about, eventually leading to cell differentiation for various functions.

At this stage, therefore, we now have primitive plant life living at or near the surface of the ocean, and animal life living at the bottom and subsisting on the dead and decaying bodies of the plants.

It must be remembered that all these forms were microscopic and exceedingly limited in their physical and physiological properties. Vast eras of time intervened before either type of organism had made very much headway, but eventually the non-photosynthetics or 'animals' had progressed to the stage of filtering lime, chalk or silica from the water to form a hard calcareous or siliceous shell surrounding the soft parts of the body. The former group, known as the Foraminifera, increased tremendously, while the latter, known as the Radiolaria, were scarcely fewer in numbers. Both groups multiplied so rapidly that before long vast areas of the sea bed were carpeted with thick deposits of the shells of these creatures, and to-day in some parts of the ocean the bed consists of layers of the shells of foraminifers or radiolarians compressed into solid rock several hundred feet thick. It can be imagined what a fantastic length of time these ocean-bed deposits must have taken to form, considering that a single foraminifer or radiolarian is as small as 0·04 mm in diameter.

Foraminifers

The beauty of form and the immense variety of the shells of these creatures has to be seen under the microscope to be believed. The word Foraminifera means 'hole-bearers', and this refers to the numbers of minute apertures in the shell which are a feature of these animals. During life the amoeba-like cell within extrudes extensions of protoplasm called *pseudopodia* ('false feet') through these holes, propelling itself along in the water by this means, and also using them to catch its food, which is, as we have seen, the minute plant life of the ocean. Fig. 2 shows some of the shell formations seen in various foraminifers.

Such protozoans as the naked amoeba, which forms no outer protective covering, are, for obvious reasons, unrepresented in the fossil record; only the hard parts of an animal remain to tell its story in the book of the rocks. We must therefore look to the groups of shell-secreting protozoans to provide us with our first evidence of protozoan existence during the dim ages when life on Earth was taking its first hesitating steps towards the greater diversity, the greater complexity, which would one day lead to the development of higher forms.

The Foraminifera provide us with our first evidence of protozoan

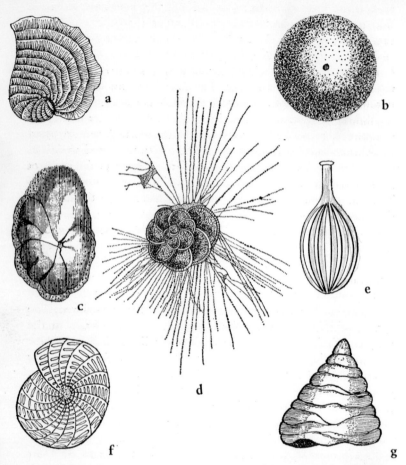

FIG. 2   Some typical foraminifers: (a) *Lagena sulcata* (×14), (b) *Orbulina universa* (×30), (c) *Rotalia veneta* (×25), (d) *Pulvinulina boueana* (×65), (e) *Peneroplis pertusus* (×14), (f) *Polyptomella crispa* (×14), (g) *Valvulina palaeotrochus* (×30)

existence in the fossil record. No Foraminifera are known from rocks earlier than the Ordovician; from that time onwards almost all limestone-type rocks can show a foraminiferous content to a greater or lesser degree, but it was the Cretaceous that saw the zenith of their development.

From the palaeontological point of view it is only the exoskeleton which requires our attention. In some cases—in fact in about one-fifth of all known foraminifers—the animal builds its skeleton by agglutinating particles of sand and other fragments; however, the majority of types have a calcareous exoskeleton, or *test*. In those cases where the test consists of carbonate of lime, there can be two types. The species of one group has a vitreous, glassy shell, covered with a reticulation of tiny holes. These holes are in reality the external openings of tiny tubes, through which the pseudopodia are extruded. The species of the other group have an opaque white shell which, under reflected light, has a porcelain-like appearance. This latter type does not have holes all over the surface, but instead there is one opening, the *oral aperture,* through which all the pseudopodia are extruded together. Foraminifers of both types are shown in Fig. 2.

A number of species have been found to have shells composed largely of aragonite. More interesting, however, is the fact that in the two groups parallel (isomorphic) development has taken place, so that some species, even whole genera, of the imperforate group closely approximate to members of the perforate group in shape, at least superficially, one group being devoid of holes, the other group being similar except for the network of apertures. It is fascinating to realise that the same kind of parallel evolution which we almost take for granted in the higher orders of the animal kingdom—for example, the marsupials of Australia and the pouched mammals which are their counterpart in South America—was already in operation at the lowest level of unicellular existence, millions of years before mammals came into being.

The simplest forms of foraminifers are spheroidal, such as *Lagena* sp. and *Orbulina* sp.—*Orbulina* means 'little globe'. These forms have no septa or internal divisions, and are therefore termed *unilocular.* Most foraminifers, however, are much more intricate, with complex series of interior chambers.

The vast majority of the foraminifers are marine, and of these a few pelagic genera are of great importance, forming what is known as the *Globigerina ooze*, a whitish or greyish mud resembling chalk in appearance, consisting of the entire or broken shells of vast uncountable millions of foraminifers. The main forms are *Globigerina, Orbulina, Hastigerina* and *Pulvinulina*, and the deposits containing them are found on the bottom of all the great oceans at depths from 600 to 2500 fathoms. The shells of these foraminifers consist of carbonate of lime, usually with some siliceous content, plus alumina, etc., in minute quantities.

The Foraminifera have contributed in no small measure to the solid crust of the Earth, and built up massive limestone formations. Almost all limestone rocks, and most calcareous shales, from the Ordovician onwards, contain large percentages of foraminifers, whose shells, visible under the microscope, are separable into various species. No foraminifers have been found in deposits earlier than Ordovician in origin.

In many species, the infiltration of glauconite (silicate of iron and potassium) prior to fossilisation has resulted in a more complete state of preservation. Some of the more recent Greensands contain the internal casts in glauconite of the shells of foraminifers, and the green grains found in many other older deposits may well prove to be of a similar nature.

In Ordovician, Silurian and Devonian strata there are few foraminifers when compared to Carboniferous foraminiferous limestones, such as the Fusulina limestones of Russia and the U.S.A. *Nummulina,* a typical Tertiary species, first appears in the Carboniferous limestone. It is still abundant, though less so, in the Permian, almost all forms resembling their Carboniferous predecessors.

In Mesozoic times, foraminifers are most abundant in the Triassic and Jurassic limestone, shale and marl systems. The white chalk deposits of the Cretaceous are composed almost exclusively of the entire or broken shells of foraminifers, *Globigerina* again playing a leading role; under the microscope the white chalk and Globigerina ooze are seen to be very similar, the main difference being that Globigerina ooze has some siliceous content, usually absent from the white chalk. The Globigerina ooze will also frequently be found to contain an admixture of the flinty shells of radiolarians (q.v.) and the siliceous spicules of sponges. A section of Globigerina ooze is shown at Fig. 3.

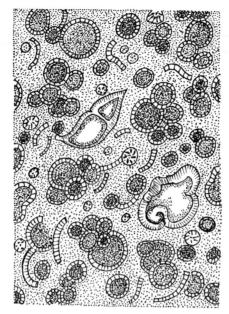

Fig. 3   A section of Globigerina ooze (× 50)

Foraminifers were varied and abundant in Tertiary times, which saw the deposition of extensive foraminiferous limestone strata, including the nummulitic limestone of Eocene origin. Later Tertiary deposits include many foraminifers now in existence.

Foraminifers, like other lowly organisms, are very persistent forms of life; even some Cretaceous species are inseparable from extant forms, and some species living to-day are believed to date from an even earlier period.

Radiolarians

Radiolarians, which form the other great group of fossil protozoans, are members of the class Rhizopoda, to which the familiar amoeba belongs. Radiolarians secrete a siliceous shell, usually of a highly-intricate reticulated pattern. The silica content of the radiolarian shell usually has the addition of a small proportion of silicate of carbon or some other organic compound of carbon.

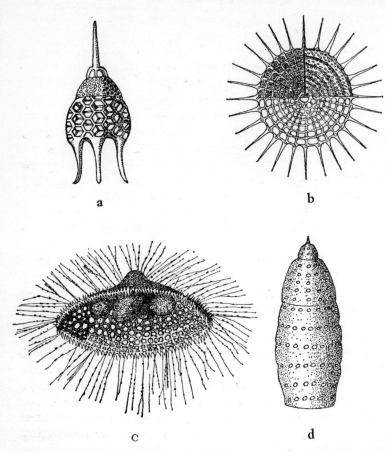

FIG. 4 Some typical radiolarians: (a) *Eucecryphalus schultzei* (×30), (b) *Stylodicta multispina* (×65), (c) *Podocyrtis schomburgi* (×65), (d) *Eucyrtidium elegans* (×65)

Radiolarians are known from very ancient times, and are abundantly represented by fossil forms. They are exclusively marine, being found in all seas, and occurring at all depths. Though mainly pelagic, some affect surface waters, while others find the various levels of the benthos a more favourable habitat; others, again, are abyssal forms. Principally they seem to occur in greatest abundance at depths between 2000 and 4000 fathoms. A greater variety of species may be found in tropical seas than in more temperate waters. Fig. 4 shows some typical Radiolarian forms.

As in the case of foraminifers, during the course of time innumerable dead bodies of radiolarians sank to the bottom, forming great deposits of a siliceous mud known as *radiolarian ooze*. All the great Mesozoic systems—the Jurassic in particular—can provide excellent examples of these deposits, such as the crypto-crystalline quartzites, which are composed mainly of the closely-compacted shells of *Spumellaria* and *Nassellaria*. Jasper, flint and chert also contain many species of radiolarians.

While few species are represented in the Cretaceous, radiolarians are widely-distributed in the Tertiary marls and clays. In the Miocene formations some of the polycystine marl deposits (known as 'Barbados earth'), which rise up to 1000 ft. above sea level, are almost exclusively composed of radiolarian shells, with a variable proportion of foraminiferous remains.

No fewer than 400 species of radiolarians are known from these beds alone, this being a conservative estimate, the figure being thought by some authorities to be nearer 500. All these strata were originally laid down as deep-sea deposits. Radiolarians from these Miocene beds include several species which are identical to forms still extant to-day in the radiolarian ooze of the deep Pacific. As in the case of their relations the foraminifers, there is little evidence of any fundamental modification or advance in radiolarian structure, function or adaptation from Palaeozoic to modern times: yet another example of the great unbroken continuity of life from earliest times to the multiplicity of living forms to-day.

3

Safety in Numbers

Some advantages of community living

IT WAS inevitable that free-living unicellular organisms could not dominate life indefinitely on the as yet unpeopled Earth, however well-protected they might be by the shells whose raw materials they had wrested from the waters. To progress at all there must be some mutual combination of forces against common enemies. True, there were no ferocious predators to contend with; not until many millions of years later was an unrelenting war to be waged against higher forms of life armed with death-dealing jaws, poison stings and other means of attack. But no less insidious, even if less visible or frightening, were adverse conditions such as lack of food, fluctuations of temperature and other climatic changes, evaporation or hyperacidity of the waters, or the encroachment of land masses through volcanic action, subsidence or other causes.

No one can be certain exactly how the first aggregation of cells took place. The most plausible theory, to my mind, is that when one of the free-living amoeboid protozoans divided by binary fission the two new individuals so formed stayed together for some physical reason instead of separating; perhaps the break between the two protoplasm-masses was almost, but not quite, complete, and the two new protozoans perforce became 'Siamese twins'. At the next stage, when each of these two in turn sub-divided, the tendency to aggregation may have been reinforced genetically, and what was once a pair of almost-joined cells now became four. The foundation was now laid for a loosely-united structure which was, in effect, a colony of similar cells. Far-fetched? I don't think so.

As isolated groups of contiguous cells developed and multiplied, the scene was gradually being set for the development of a new phylum of animals whose bodies would at first consist merely of groups of loosely-connected similar cells, perhaps irregular in their disposition to start with, which would gradually expand into colonies exhibiting a more marked degree of organisation, albeit at a very primitive level. With the consequent increase in size of these colonies, the next logical stage would be the formation of some kind of hardened skeletal framework, built up from elements extracted from the waters, which was essential in order to support and protect the soft, vulnerable jelly-like mass of protoplasm which constituted the living body. The Porifera, or sponges, are the culmination of just such a sequence of developmental stages.

The Porifera (sponges)

The Porifera (literally 'pore-bearers') or sponges, once thought to be plants, are now universally accepted as constituting the phylum of animals placed between the protozoans, or unicellular organisms, and the coelenterates, whose bodies consist of two layers of cells.

Certain sponges have cells with amoeboid affinities; the cells found in some other species resemble flagellated infusoria. It is therefore hardly surprising that, once the idea that sponges were 'plants' was finally relinquished, the biologists of the day thought that they were colonial protozoans. The definition now usually adopted is that sponges are multicellular organisms whose cells are typically disposed to form an outer and an inner layer, separated by an intermediate stratum. In this particular they bear a more than superficial resemblance to the coelenterates; but here the similarity ends. Although, again, these layers are traversed by series of canals opening to the exterior (cf. medusoids), the cell aggregations in the Porifera are supported by a rigid framework of siliceous or calcareous needle-like structures called *spicules*—a feature never found in the coelenterate body. It is this framework which remains, after the living protoplasm has disintegrated, to tell the story. Some fossil sponge forms are shown in Plates 1–3.

There is no buccal orifice, gut, or anus, nor anything even remotely analogous to a nervous system such as the nematoblasts of coelenterates (which could be defined as the most rudimentary form of a primitive nervous network found in the animal kingdom).

The function of the canals in sponges is to conduct water into and out of the body through the framework, thus enabling oxygen to reach all parts of the body, and collectively these canals form the *aqueferous system*. In some species only one of these external openings, called the *osculum*, is employed for the expulsion of water after its oxygen has been extracted, all the other openings conveying water into the body only; this system is very easily observed in the common 'loofah' bath sponge, which is covered with pores of minute size, but has one large osculum at the anterior end. Another example of a sponge of this type, the Cretaceous *Ventriculites striatus*, is shown at Fig. 5. Some other types of sponge, however, have more than one osculum, though these are in the minority.

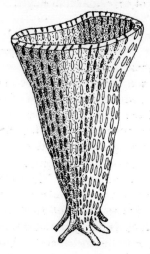

FIG. 5   *Ventriculites striatus*, a Cretaceous sponge (× ⅓)

Flagellate cells in the interior drive water (i.e., oxygen) further into the body; this having been accomplished, they drive water out again, this time excreting waste carbon dioxide to the exterior.

The common bath 'loofah' is an exception to the usual pattern of siliceous or calcareous spicules, in that the framework is fibrous, being composed of a hard, horny substance called *keratode spongin*. Most sponges, however, are of the more usual spiculated type. In the groups whose spicules are composed of silica, the spicules may either be embedded in a fibrous skeleton, or the latter may be devoid of horny fibres. In the groups whose spicules are calcareous, however, there is never any fibrous or horny extraneous material in the skeleton. Some types of spicules commonly found in sponges are shown at Fig. 6.

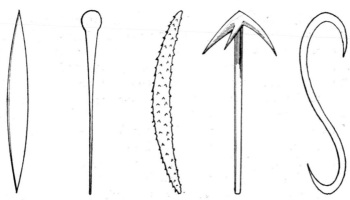

Fig. 6   Some typical sponge spicules (× 80)

The distribution of sponges is predominantly marine; fresh-water species are so few as to be negligible. Of the marine species, with which we are concerned, three sub-groups occur only in shallow seas, all the rest being found at depths ranging from 100 to 2500 fathoms.

Some of the siliceous sponges have undergone chemical trans-formation during fossilisation, the silica changing to an amorphous colloidal state, during which process it loses its original glassy appearance and becomes porcellanous, appearing milky-white under reflected light. Some of these metamorphosed spicules may exhibit some colour refraction under polarised light. In extreme cases silica may pass through several changes; from the crystalline or cryptocrystalline form it becomes colloidal in nature and can form a type of quartz or chalcedony. Colloidal silica is extremely vulnerable to chemical activity, and is stable only in crystalline form. There is, however, a tendency to pass from the unstable colloid to the crystalline condition; under favourable conditions this has occurred without destroying the form of the skeleton or framework of the sponge.

Some of the siliceous fossil sponges turn up from time to time as hollow casts in the matrix of the enclosing rock owing to the dis-solution of the silica; this is also a fairly common phenomenon in the case of calcareous sponges. The hollow space has gradually filled up with mineral deposits extracted by water from the matrix rock; a *pseudomorph*, or model of the original specimen, is then formed, consisting most commonly of crystalline calcite, though other pseudomorphs may be made of iron peroxide, iron pyrites or glauconite. Very occasionally a fossil sponge may be found in which one portion has been preserved in its original state and the remainder in modified form. Horny, unspiculated sponges are never represented pseudomorphically.

The skeletons of siliceous spiculated sponges have been discovered in rocks as ancient as those of Cambrian origin. The oldest known sponge is *Protospongia fenestrata,* from the Menevian Slate of South Wales. It is not uncommonly found also in Ordovician strata, in which two groups of sponges are represented. The Silurian period shows the same two groups, or their representatives, plus the appearance of one more new group.

By Devonian times sponges showed a sharp decline both in variety of species and in numbers, but this was merely the lull before the storm, as it were, for in the ensuing Carboniferous period there was a sudden upsurge of Porifera, with five distinct subgroups containing vast numbers of species. Thick beds of chert were formed in Carboniferous times from the gradual accumulation of siliceous spicules on the bottom of shallow seas.

Enormous numbers of sponges, divided into three distinct groups, characterised Jurassic times. The first freshwater genus occurred at this period, and its remains may be found in the Purbeck beds. The same three groups persisted into the Cretaceous (except the Upper Cretaceous), vast numbers of new species occurring.

The beds of siliceous rock characteristic of the Upper and Lower Greensands were formed by the accumulation of microscopic sponge spicules. Various species contributed to these deposits, in some of which the spicules are loosely compacted, giving rise to a porous siliceous rock, while in others the silica was dissolved by the action of salt water and redeposited, mixing with unchanged spicules to form chert (see Fig. 7). Nodular flints from the White Chalk were formed by the dissolution of the skeletons of flinty sponges, redeposited in the form of solid silica.

The Porifera started to decline in Tertiary times, several types becoming extinct, until by modern times comparatively few types remain extant when compared with the proliferation of species during Mesozoic times.

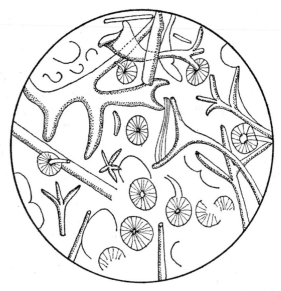

FIG. 7   Section of chert from Upper Greensands, showing sponge spicules embedded in chalcedonic matric (× 30)

The Coelenterates

The Coelenterata, or diploblastic animals, are characterised by having two layers of cells separated by a jelly-like mesogloea, and a hollow body cavity or coelom, from which the phylum derives its name. Represented to-day by the Hydrozoa (e.g., Hydra and the jellyfishes) and the Actinozoa (corals and sea-anemones), the group's modern representatives are far inferior in numbers to their ancient forbears which, from Ordovician times onwards, included some very important and abundant forms such as the now extinct Graptolites and Stromatoporoids, which have no close relatives now in existence; while the Ctenophora or comb-jellies, whose living representatives are well-known to-day, have no hard parts and so they are not represented in the fossil record, leaving a gap in our knowledge which may be bridged only by conjecture, based on our knowledge of allied forms and of their modern descendants.

Almost all coelenterates, both ancient and modern, are marine, except for the well-known freshwater Hydra, so beloved by biology teachers. Unfortunately these soft-bodied forms have left no traces in the fossil record, though we may be pretty certain, from all the available evidence, that they were represented in some form or another.

The earliest known remains of coelenterates occur in the rock-systems of the Upper Cambrian, these ancient forms including hydroids and graptolites. By Ordovician times, however, the Actinozoa, or corals, had appeared and were already exhibiting great variation in form, which would lead us to believe that this group of animals had developed very early in time. From the Ordovician onwards the coelenterates were very abundant, and two important classes, the Thecaphora (graptolites) and the Stromatoporoidea, loomed large on the Ordovician horizon. Of other groups such as the Ctenophora we have far less knowledge as, being wholly devoid of hard parts, they have left scarcely a trace in the fossil record, apart from impressions in the sand here and there which were fortuitously preserved as the sand gradually became compressed into a layer of solid rock.

Not only did the graptolites and stromatoporoids become extinct, but their fossilised remains are restricted wholly to rocks of Devonian age and older. The freshwater hydra, if it, or some ancestor, existed in Palaeozoic times, is wholly absent from the fossil record.

A sub-group of very ancient origin allied to Hydra is the Thecaphora, in which the body takes the form of a colonial polypoid, the individual polyps being united by a common stem or *coenosarc*. The base of this structure is fixed to a substratum by an adherent basal disc or *hydrorrhiza*. A chitinous outer covering encloses not only the coenosarc but also each individual polyp, giving the latter a some-what cup-like appearance; these individual polyps are known as *hydrothecae*. Some of these grow larger than the others and produce reproductive bodies (*zooids* or *gonophores*), the polyps giving rise to them being known as *gonothecae*.

The existing Thecaphora are widely represented and even abundant in modern seas, but although represented in the early Palaeozoic deposits, members of this group have not come to light in any of the Mesozoic or early Cenozoic strata. This unexplained gap is the more puzzling when we take into consideration the hard chitinous covering, which lends itself well to preservation. One feels, on the evidence offered by evolution, that it is hardly likely that a group could flourish, become extinct for millions of years, and then suddenly reappear to take up the threads again, as it were, and resume where it had left off; evolution just does not work that way! One can only assume that somewhere there are some unexplored deposits containing Mesozoic and subsequent thecaphorans still awaiting discovery; after all, despite the intensive interest in, and study of, palaeontology during the last hundred years, it is hardly feasible that palaeontologists could have dug up and examined all the strata underlying the entire crust of the Earth . . .

At this juncture I must mention briefly in passing the interesting structures known as 'medusites', from the Cambrian rocks of Sweden. The Swedish palaeontologist Nathorst, who first discovered and named them, considered them to have been formed by the filling in with mud or sand of the body cavities of dead jellyfishes, forming a cast of the coelenteron of the medusoid. Nathorst pointed out that many modern jellyfishes are known to have a habit of lying on the bottom with the mouth upwards, a position which would, of course, facilitate the filling up of the coelenteron with any muddy or sandy sediment which drifted along. Furthermore, Nathorst has shown that structures almost identical in form and markings to the Cambrian 'medusites' may be made artificially by taking plaster of Paris casts of the body cavities of modern jellyfishes.

The Graptolites

The Graptolites are extinct Hydrozoa, all the known forms of which were confined to the Upper Cambrian, Ordovician, Silurian and Devonian strata. They belong to the class Thecaphora.

The Graptolites may be defined as composite Hydrozoans, whose polyps were united by a single coenosarc which was enclosed in a chitinous tubular external covering. The individual polyps were further protected by separate hydrothecae. Unlike the groups we have discussed above, however, the graptolites were free-swimming organisms, and the body was furnished with a small structure called the *sicula*, usually lanceolate or triangular in shape. This is thought by some authorities to represent an embryonic skeleton.

The young immature graptolite at first consisted of little more than this sicula, which housed the embryo coenosarc. A rod-like axis, called the *virgula*, then developed along its entire length, in many species projecting at one or both extremities.

In the next stage a bud, consisting of the first hydrotheca containing a polyp, appeared on one side, the next bud forming on the opposite side; and so on. The virgula was probably hollow, and supported the chitinous skeleton. It runs along the dorsal side opposite the hydrothecae, and lies outside the coenosarc proper. The hydrothecae vary enormously in form, and usually overlap one another (see Fig. 8).

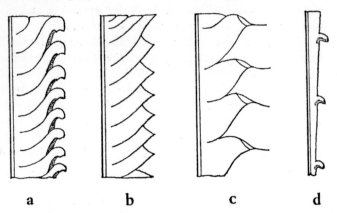

a   b   c   d

FIG. 8   Forms of hydrothecae in graptolites (× 55): (a) *Monograptus clingani*, (b) *Monograptus colonus*, (c) *Monograptus spinigerus*, (d) *Monograptus hisingeri*

One of the most interesting of these ancient thecaphorans is the Upper Cambrian *Dendrograptus*, in which the organism had the form of a branching frond provided with a substantial coenosarc whereby, presumably, it was attached to a substratum. The chitinous cups, or hydrothecae, differed from those of most other forms by not overlapping (see Fig. 9).

In the Silurian *Dictyonema retiforme* (Fig. 10) we have a type resembling *Dendrograptus* but devoid (apparently) of a coenosarc. It is not certain whether *Dictyonema* was attached to a substratum or to a floating weed, but the evidence points to its having been fixed, as the branches all radiate from a common base. Further species of *Dictyonema* evolved into the middle Devonian, and these later forms bear a striking resemblance to the Fenestellae or 'lace-corals', which belong to the Polyzoa and have a calcareous skeleton; they also have no hydrothecae.

FIG. 9 *Dendrograptus hallianus* ($\times \frac{4}{5}$)

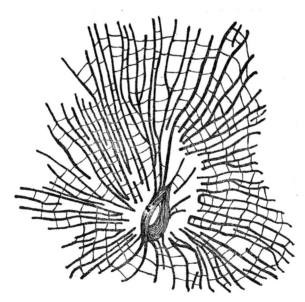

FIG. 10 *Dictyonema retiforme* (after Hall) ($\times \frac{2}{3}$)

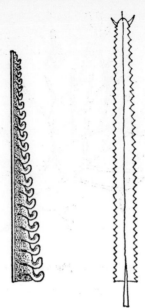

FIG. 11   (a) *Monograptus priodon*, (b) *Diplograptus foliaceus* (both slightly
enlarged)

Some graptolites were single in form, as *Monograptus priodon*
(Fig. 11a). All the single graptolites are confined to the Upper
Silurian. Others, such as *Diplograptus foliaceus,* had a double row of
hydrothecae attached to what at first sight appears to be a single
virgula, but which actually consists of two separate rods in close
dorsal apposition (Fig. 11b). Graptolites of this type are Ordovician

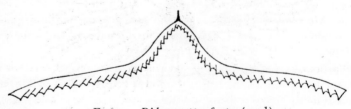

FIG. 12   *Didymograptus fractus* ($\times 1\frac{1}{2}$)

FIG. 13   *Dimorphograptus* sp. (×4)

in origin. The 'twin' types such as *Didymograptus* are characterised by having two separate series of hydrothecae, each supported by its own virgula and attached at the proximal extremity to a common coenosarc (Fig. 12). All these forms are found in Upper Cambrian and Ordovician deposits, the type genus *Didymograptus* itself being confined to the Ordovician.

The reproductive processes in graptolites were similar to those in the hydroid zoophytes, in which gonophores were produced in larger gonothecae, and gave rise to zooids (reproductive bodies).

A remarkable graptolite is *Dimorphograptus* (Fig. 13), in which the proximal portion bears the characteristics of the 'double-edged' group, while distally it branches out into the two arms of a 'twin' type. Morphologically this graptolite, which is of Silurian origin, more closely approaches *Monograptus* in the possession of adherent sicula.

Particular types of graptolites have been shown to be characteristic of specific horizons in the Upper Cambrian, Ordovician and Silurian rock-systems, making them very important as index fossils, about which more will be said later.

The Stromatoporoids

The Stromatoporoids form a large and important class of extinct coelenterates whose remains are confined to Ordovician, Silurian and Devonian rock-systems. The Stromatoporoids, which sometimes reached a considerable size, secreted a limy skeleton, and it is these skeletons that largely make up some of the Silurian and Devonian limestones.

The pattern of growth in stromatoporoids was extremely variable, but the most typical form was spheroidal, the body being attached to a substratum. In some cases the skeleton was dendroid in form, but all the known species have one common feature—the skeleton is composed of conspicuous concentric calcareous layers or laminae, separated by narrow spaces. At right angles to these laminae are radial rod-like structures, and the whole arrangement gives rise to the typical reticulated appearance. On the external surface of the body were numerous minute pores opening internally into the first sub-superficial interlaminar cavity. Some authorities take the view that the zooids of the colony were liberated through these pores to the exterior, though owing to the almost microscopic size of the pores it would probably be more logical to suppose that they served a respiratory purpose rather than a reproductive function.

The under-surface of the body is concave, and in many species size-able spaces occur not only between the laminae themselves but also around the point of attachment to the substratum. These spaces open to the interior and it might well be conjectured that zooids would be able to make their way to the outside via these spaces from the interior of the body. So far as is at present known, the zooids were produced anywhere along the laminae, and there is no stromatoporoid as yet discovered to have had specific gonophores or other zooid-producing bodies at any particular point.

The Stromatoporoids can be sub-divided into two great groups. In the first group, of which *Actinostroma* may be taken as the type genus, the skeleton is composed of concentric laminae intersected by radial rods which remain separate and do not become fused with one another to form a continuous network. The earliest types of *Actinostroma* occur in the Silurian deposits, but the genus attained its zenith in the Devonian.

The second group, which ranged from the Ordovician to the Devonian, with *Labechia* as the type, has a different appearance (see Fig. 14). The external surface is more tubercular than pitted, and the basal attachment mechanism is attenuated into a peduncle. A calcareous membrane, the *epitheca,* covers the underside of the body, and the calcareous laminae of the interior are cuneiform in shape. Although the radial rods are hollow, it is noteworthy that there appears to be no exit at either end: a puzzling feature indeed. Where were the zooids discharged from the interior? Was there an external coenosarc, from which gonothecae budded off and released zooids? This would seem to be the only plausible explanation.

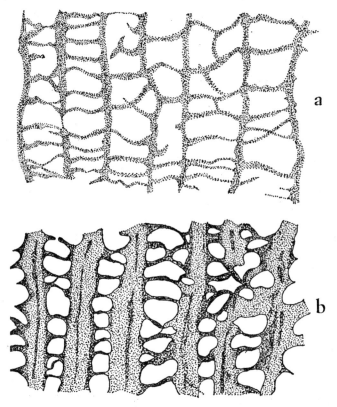

FIG. 14   Structure of stromatoporoids (× 12): (a) Vertical section of *Actinostroma,* (b) Vertical section of *Labechia*

The Hydrocorallines

Two sub-groups of marine Hydrozoa which secrete a regular skeleton of carbonate of lime, formerly referred to the true corals, are now classified as the Hydrocorallines. The well-known *Millepora,* which means '(bearing) a thousand pores', is the typical genus of the first group (the Milleporidae), and contributed largely to the formation of coral reefs in various regions. The calcareous skeleton, or *coenosteum,* is usually of a laminated or foliaceous form, but in some species it is simply branched. Two series of vertical tubes, which contained the zooids, open to the exterior by apertures of two distinct sizes, the larger being termed *gastropores* and the smaller *dactylopores* (see Fig. 15). These may be irregularly distributed, or the dactylopores may be arranged in a more or less definite system around the gastropores.

It has been shown that these two series of tubes gave rise to larger and smaller zooids respectively, which differed both in structure and function. The larger zooids, or *gastrozooids,* possessed a mouth and a coelom or digestive cavity, and had from four to six short tentacles. The smaller zooids, or *dactylozooids,* which had no buccal orifice, possessed short club-shaped lateral tentacles. Both kinds of zooidal tubes are intersected internally by distinct transverse calcareous partitions called *tabulae* (see Fig. 16), but there are no traces of radiating vertical partitions or septa. The entire coenosteum is composed of thin concentric laminae. The reproductive process in *Millepora* is imperfectly known.

The earliest known forms appear in the Eocene rocks; one Cretaceous genus, *Porosphaera,* which was formerly considered to be related to *Millepora,* has recently been re-classified as being more nearly referable to the true Sponges.

The second group of the Hydrocorallines is the Stylasteridae, none of which has been discovered in deposits of more ancient origin than the Trias. All of them are marine, with a wide range of distribution, some having been inhabitants of shallow coastal waters, while others occurred at great depths.

The coenosteum of the Stylasteridae is calcareous, usually dendroid in form. Many of them bear rounded apertures on the surface which have the appearance of being intersected marginally by radiating partitions or septa, superficially resembling the madreporian corals. In other species the surface shows a series of large

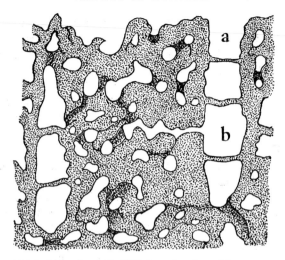

FIG. 15 Vertical section of *Millepora* showing (a) gastropores, (b) dactylopores (× 35)

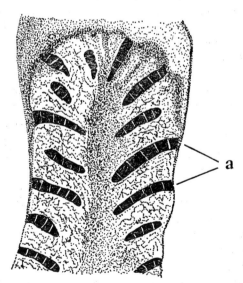

FIG. 16 Vertical section of *Millepora* showing tabulae (a) (× 40)

apertures, interspersed irregularly by smaller openings. The coenosteum is composed of sub-crystalline calcareous tissue traversed in all directions by a branched canal system. The zooids were again of two kinds, as in *Millepora*.

Besides the Triassic forms referred to earlier, species of this group have been found in Tertiary strata. Certain Cretaceous forms, at present imperfectly known, are probably referable to this group.

The Actinozoa (corals and sea-anemones)

The animals which comprise this group are definable as coelenterates in which the buccal orifice opens into an oesophageal tube, which in turn leads into the coelom or body cavity. The oesophagus is separated from the body wall by an intervening space which is divided into a series of compartments by radiating vertical membranous partitions called *mesenteries*, to which the reproductive organs are attached. In these two particulars the Actinozoa differ fundamentally from the Hydrozoa, which are devoid of an oesophagus and whose coelom has no mesenteric subdivisions. Some fossil corals are shown in Plates 4–6.

The body wall of the Actinozoa consists, as in all coelenterates, of an external *ectoderm*, an internal *endoderm* and an intermediate layer of jelly-like material, the *mesogloea*. The ectoderm is prolonged inwards at the buccal orifice to form the oesophageal lining, while the coelomic lining is formed from the endoderm.

Actinozoans may be simple, as the sea-anemones which consist of a single polyp, or composite, as in the colonial corals, consisting of numerous polyps united by a common coenosarc. In the sea-anemones the buccal orifice is surrounded by a series of muscular tentacles, while the opposite end attaches the animal by a basal disc to the substratum, to which it clings by suction. A typical sea-anemone is shown at Fig. 17. The bodies of sea-anemones are soft, and so these animals have left very few traces in the fossil record; but the corals, of course, are a very different story, since they secrete hard calcareous structures.

The hard parts of corals vary a great deal according to family. Some merely produce free spicules of carbonate of lime embedded in their soft parts (see Fig. 18), which do not unite to form a coherent skeleton; the Alcyonarians form a typical group of this type. In another group, the organ-pipe corals or Tubipora, these spicules

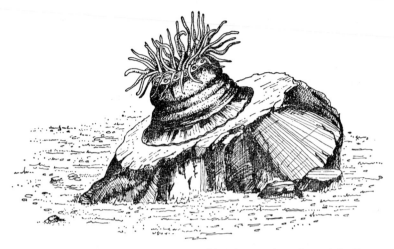

FIG. 17   A typical sea-anemone *(Actinia mesembryanthemum)* (× ⅘)

fuse with one another to form a coherent external skeleton. In another type, *Corallium,* one of the rugose corals, the spicules fuse to form a solid cylindrical calcareous axis in the centre of the coenosarc.

In the great majority of Actinozoa, however, the calcareous skeleton is not formed by the fusion of spicules but is the result of the secretion of carbonate of lime at the outer surface of the ecto-derm; corals of this type are termed *sclerodermic,* and the actual calcareous tissue is known as the *sclerenchyma.*

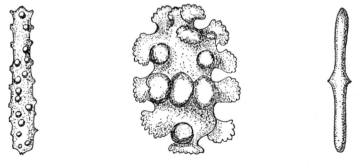

FIG. 18   Calcareous spicules (dermosclerites) of corals (× 80)

By the process of budding the colony grows until gradually with the passage of time vast coral reefs may be formed covering many square miles in area and hundreds of miles in length, such as the Great Barrier Reef of Australia. Corals also reproduce by fission, in which one polyp divides longitudinally to form two, but these two are never completely separated from one another and remain united at the base. Each new 'Siamese twin' polyp, however, secretes its own calcareous skeleton, thus increasing the size of the colony. The commencement of fission in a polyp is marked by the development of an internal vertical partition, which at first is incomplete. A corresponding partition then develops opposite the first one, and by the inward growth and final joining of these the polyp is ultimately divided into two.

The Actinozoa fall naturally into four sub-groups, the first of which, the Zoantharia, is largely represented by living forms. All are marine, some inhabiting shallow seas and others being denizens of the deep oceans. All the great coral reefs were formed in shallow tropical waters.

At this juncture it must be pointed out that the 'coral reefs' found in modern seas are not composed entirely and exclusively of corals, either living or dead. Although corals are the principal agents in reef-formation, other organisms which secrete a calcareous skeleton have also played a not inconsiderable part. Accumulations of the calcareous skeletons of hydrocorallines and molluscs, as well as of calcareous algae, form a large proportion of the underlying deposits; it must also be realised that only a portion—mainly the outer edges—of a modern coral reef is actually composed of living corals. Finally, the materials which make up a coral reef are liable to undergo various changes caused by the continual percolation of the water; these changes in many cases involve complete crystallisation, with consequent obliteration of the original organic structure of the rock.

Coralline limestones have been formed during all the great geological periods from the Ordovician onwards. However, the original *form* of any ancient coral reef can hardly be more than a matter of inference. The changes wrought by displacements and denudations which have occurred subsequent to the original formation of the reef have continued for such long periods that it must always be perilous to treat any existing outcrop of coralline limestone as representing the original boundaries of an old coral reef. On this account there is much uncertainty concerning the so-called 'atolls' which have been described as occurring in rocks of Devonian or Carboniferous age. It is highly improbable that an 'atoll' of such great antiquity should have so far escaped destruction by denudation that its original form should still be preserved; this is still further borne out by the fact that these 'atolls' have invariably occurred in areas which are known to have undergone extensive disturbance.

4

The Ascendancy of the Trilobites

Variety within a single group

TRILOBITES are probably the most familiar of all the smaller fossils, and in this chapter this particular class of the phylum Arthropoda will be discussed. This phylum includes not only the trilobites but embraces the lobsters, crabs, king-crabs, barnacles, crayfish, shrimps—in fact animals of this phylum range in size from the almost microscopic Daphnia or so-called water-flea to the extinct gigantic Eurypterids, which sometimes reached a length of twelve feet. Clearly, to attempt to describe even a few representatives only of every order contained within the framework of such a huge and diverse phylum is beyond the scope of a book of this size, so we shall have to content ourselves with a brief résumé of the trilobites, which form one of the most well-known of fossil groups.

Characteristics of arthropods

The Trilobita form one of the six great sub-divisions of the phylum Arthropoda or jointed-legged animals, which are defined by zoologists as having the body composed of a series of somites or segments, usually definite in number according to the particular animals concerned. Each segment is usually provided with a pair of appendages, which are always jointed, although the actual number of joints may vary. Both the segmented body and the jointed appendages are usually covered by a chitinous integument or *exoskeleton*. Muscles extend from the body into the interior of the appendages, and the nervous system consists typically of a chain of *ganglia* or nerve-centres extending along the ventral surface of the body. If a heart is present, it is situated dorsally. Respiration is carried out either by means of gills or tracheae, though in a few terrestrial families there may be tubular involutions of the integument to form pulmonary sacs adapted for breathing air.

All six classes of arthropods are represented in very early rocks, the Crustacea and Trilobita being already differentiated far back into Cambrian times, while the other three classes are known to exist from Silurian deposits. The point of divergence of the six great groups of the Arthropoda must therefore have occurred long before early Cambrian times, and it would seem highly improbable that we shall ever know with any degree of even reasonable certainty any details of the primitive stock from which the jointed-legged animals originally arose.

The trilobite body

Animals of the class Trilobita (three-lobed animals) may be defined as essentially aquatic creatures provided with gills or branchiae for extracting oxygen from the water; their exoskeleton must of necessity be water-resistant. The body segments are usually definite in number, most of them carrying paired jointed appendages. Two pairs of antennae are carried on the head; some of the anterior pairs of appendages are modified into biting jaws, and a varying number of paired legs are attached to some of the abdominal somites. The chitinous exoskeleton may in some cases be partly calcified. Some tribolites are shown in Plates 7–9.

The body of a typical trilobite may be divided into three parts— the head, the thorax and the abdomen, each of these three subdivisions usually comprising a fixed number of segments. In some cases the head and thorax are united to form a *cephalothorax*, which may be covered by a hard *carapace* or protective shield. Sometimes there is a caudal shield, the *pygidium*, at the extremity of the abdomen. Eyes may or may not be present, but where occurring are two in number, usually compound, and set symmetrically in the anterior part of the cephalothorax. They may be sessile, i.e. set directly into the head, or they may be carried at the tips of the stalk-like peduncles; in fact this distinction serves to differentiate between the two main groups, the *Hedriophthalmata*, or sessile-eyed group, and the *Podophthalmata* or pedunculate-eyed group.

All the foregoing perhaps somewhat tedious anatomical details have been necessary in order to prepare the ground for an understanding of how the living trilobite was made up. Trilobites belong to the sub-order Branchiopoda ('gill-footed' animals), in which the respiratory branchiae are attached to the legs; in some cases the legs themselves are adapted for respiration by themselves becoming flattened branchiae. The legs are used for swimming as well as crawling along the bottom, and the body may be either naked or it may be protected by a hard carapace, which may enclose either the entire body or the head and thorax only.

The trilobites are typical of Palaeozoic rocks, and are easily distinguished by their trilobate (three-lobed) form, common to all the exceedingly numerous species. Head, thorax and abdomen are distinct, the head, which is covered by a cephalic shield, bearing a pair of compound eyes. Jointed legs with attached branchiae are carried by both thoracic and abdominal somites. A calcareous shell or 'crust' covers the entire dorsal surface of the body, and a caudal shield or pygidium is present.

The eyes of trilobites exhibit remarkable diversity. The facets, which are covered by a thin cornea, may range in number from 14 to as many as 15,000 in each eye. Four genera *(Agnostus, Ampyx, Trinucleus* and *Conocephalus)* are eyeless.

Although the typical form of the fossil trilobite looks rigid, it must be remembered that in life the flexibility of the thoracic and abdominal somites was such that the animal could roll itself up, after the manner of a hedgehog. The number of thoracic segments varies from as few as two *(Agnostus)* to as many as 26 *(Harpes)* or more. Even the pygidium may sometimes consist of as many as 28 segments *(Amphion)*, though two is the more usual number.

The ventral surfaces of trilobites have only rarely been preserved, and our knowledge of this part of the creature's anatomy is still very incomplete. In the exceedingly rare specimens which have been preserved showing these details, five-jointed limbs with branchial filaments are clearly present, and are carried by all the body segments from thorax to pygidium. On each side of the thorax there is also a row of gill-like appendages, and the four pairs of cephalic appendages are all modified to form jaws.

Trilobites laid eggs, spheroidal in shape, each measuring from 0·5 mm to 1 mm in diameter; they appear to have been deposited in clusters. The larval forms of trilobites are known only from a few examples, and in these the body appears to have been naked.

Trilobites were, as far as we are able to ascertain, mud- and bottom-dwellers, and must have frequented particular localities in incredible numbers. Certain tracks and markings in the rocks where trilobites commonly occur are attributed to their movements across the muddy bottom of their habitat. Some of these tracks are of a considerable size, and many of them are very similar in appearance to the tracks made by the *Limulus*, which is their nearest living relative. There are, however, various striking differences as well as similarities between the anatomy of *Limulus* and that of its long-extinct relations.

Trilobites are exclusively Palaeozoic, their range extending from

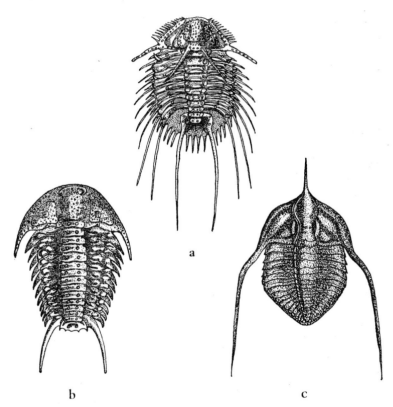

FIG. 19 Some typical trilobites (× ⅔): (a) *Cheirurus pleurexanthemus*, (b) *Acidaspis dufrenoyi* (after Zittel), (c) *Ampyx nudus* (after Salter)

the Lower Cambrian to the Permian and attaining the peak of their development in the Ordovician and Silurian rocks. Their decline had already set in during the Devonian period; by Carboniferous times only four genera remained, and from the Permian only one form, a species of the genus *Phillipsia,* is known. Some typical trilobites are shown at Fig. 19.

5

The Problematical Echinoderms

Chordate affinities?

ONE of the most important aspects of evolution is the search for the exact point of divergence which gave rise to the chordates, the phylum which embraces all the vertebrates, including ourselves.

The three distinctive features shared by chordate animals are the possession of a longitudinal cartilaginous rod-like supporting structure, the *notochord* (which in the higher forms is replaced by the vertebral column), a dorsal nerve-system, and gill-slits. These structures are invariably present in the embryo even if they may be modified or lost in later life. Most chordates are bilaterally symmetrical and have a relatively complex digestive and excretory system.

The simplest and most primitive chordates, which form the sub-phylum Acraniata, are devoid of a brain or skull, but the three typical features of notochord, dorsal nerve-system and gill-slits are nevertheless invariably present. Examples of these lowly creatures are amphioxus, the sea-squirts or tunicates, and the so-called acorn-worms or tongue-worms *(Balanoglossus)*. All other chordates possess a brain protected by a skull or cranium, on account of which they are grouped together in the sub-phylum Craniata. The body is supported by a segmented vertebral column or backbone, and the sub-phylum includes such diverse classes as the fishes, amphibians, reptiles, birds and mammals, including man. The fishes outnumber twenty to one all the other vertebrates put together.

The notochord is derived from the primitive endoderm and, as stated above, is present in the embryos of all chordates, including man. The only vertebrates in which the notochord persists into post-foetal life are the jawless fishes such as lampreys and certain groups of jawed fishes, in which the vertebral column forms around it; more will be said about these in the appropriate chapters. In all other vertebrates the notochord is replaced altogether by the vertebral column by the time the embryo is fully-developed and ready to leave the parent body.

The second most important chordate characteristic is the dorsal nerve-system, which is present in all chordates without exception from amphioxus to man. In other animals which are not chordates, such as earthworms and insects, the nervous system is situated ventrally, or even laterally in a few cases, but never dorsally.

The third distinctive chordate feature is the presence of gill-slits. In the lower forms such as amphioxus and fishes these structures are present throughout life and form a complete respiratory system, but in the higher vertebrates gill-slits are present only in the embryo. (In the human embryo gill-pouches develop, but these do not actually become perforated to form gill-slits).

The more primitive the chordate the greater the number of gill-slits. The embryo amphioxus has about 60 pairs of gill-slits, which increase in number as the animal grows. A large and indefinite number of gill-slits is always indicative of a primitive condition; in sharks, for example, there are always only six gill-slits.

The puzzle of the tunicates

The tunicates, or sea-squirts, bear about as little resemblance to the conventional notion of a chordate as is possible to imagine; yet latterly zoologists have, on studying these lowly creatures, been drawn more and more irresistibly to the conclusion that somewhere along the line there is some relationship, however obscure, between the structure of these animals and that of the higher chordates.

The tunicates have always been previously classified as echinoderms along with the more familiar starfishes, brittle-stars, holothuroids, sea-urchins, crinoids and their kin. The tunicates are so named because the ectoderm is a tough, tunic-like integument; their common name of sea-squirt derives from their habit of contracting the body violently when disturbed, which has the effect of suddenly ejecting the internal water. This water is squirted out in twin streams from the two openings in the body, the mouth and the atrium (a primitive form of cloaca). Some tunicates are free-swimming, but others remain permanently attached to a substratum such as rock, or seaweed. The animals are hermaphrodite (i.e., they contain male and female organs in the same body), and they are remarkable for their circulatory system, in which the heart pumps the blood round the body in one direction for several beats and then reverses this action.

Looking at an adult tunicate, it will be seen that the animal is furnished with gill-slits, but there is no sign of any structure even remotely resembling either a notochord or a dorsal nerve-system. The presence of gill-slits alone is of course no indication of chordate affinities; as we have seen, the trilobites and other crustaceans have gill-slits in abundance, but no one could by any stretch of the imagination visualise them to be chordates. How, then, did the zoologists who were studying the tunicates connect them with the chordates and find in them any reason to suggest re-classifying them in the same phylum with amphioxus and fishes?

As the tunicate life-history was studied in more detail, it was discovered that it had a free-swimming larval form not unlike a tadpole in appearance. It had a tail for swimming, and gill-slits for respiration; this latter feature could be expected in the juvenile stage of an animal which breathed by means of gills in adult life. However, dissection brought a shock discovery: the larval tunicate had *a distinct and unmistakable notochord and a well-developed dorsal nerve-system*! It lost these two features as it entered the adult stage of its life-cycle, just as many primitive features present in the vertebrate embryo are lost on full development being attained prior to birth or hatching from the egg.

Was this the breakthrough so long awaited by biologists? Are the lowly sea-squirts the ancestral stock from which the higher chordates eventually developed? It is fascinating puzzles like these which make the study of evolution so absorbing, knowing as we do that for every exciting discovery of this nature we make there are dozens of other surprises awaiting us.

The acorn-worms

The acorn-worms or tongue-worms now deserve brief mention. These primitive marine worms have well-defined gill-slits, but their 'notochord' (if, indeed, it is such) is very imperfectly-developed; it is a short rod-like structure at the anterior end of the body only. In the matter of a nerve-system the acorn-worm seems to have the best of both worlds: there are *two* distinct and separate nerve-cords, one dorsal and one ventral—a type of nerve-system location found in no other animal, either vertebrate or invertebrate.

However obscure the possibility of chordate affinities being 'read into' these features of the adult acorn-worm, the larval stage is almost indistinguishable in appearance from the juvenile stages of certain echinoderms. Because of this many biologists are not yet able to accept that the acorn-worms are true chordates, but we shall not, I feel, be accused of being unrealistic if we incline towards the view that the acorn-worms may be close to the ancestral forms from which the first true and undisputed chordates originated.

Echinoderms past and present

Echinoderms ('spiny-skinned' animals) include some of the most exquisitely-coloured and delicate of all marine animals. They include both free-living and attached forms, and live at varying depths. The phylum is sub-divided into five classes represented by living forms: the starfishes, the ophiuroids or brittle-stars, the Echinoidea or sea-urchins, the holothuroids or sea-cucumbers, and the crinoids or sea-lilies; and two extinct classes, the cystoids and the blastoids. Of these the first-named four groups are free-living and belong to the sub-phylum Eleutherozoa; the last-named three groups are usually fixed to the seabed by a jointed calcareous stalk-like peduncle and belong to the sub-phylum Pelmatozoa.

Crinoids, which are very abundant fossils, were thought to be extinct until about 70 years ago when a deep-sea expedition hauled up more than 10,000 living crinoids in a single operation! Many living crinoids are brilliantly-coloured; most are gregarious and live in large colonies whose delicate, flower-like beauty has led to their being referred to as 'the gardens of the sea'. Perfectly-preserved bud-like forms of incredible beauty are not uncommon in Lower Carboniferous limestones; I once found one exposed at the surface of a rock forming part of a wall along a country lane not far from Matlock in Derbyshire.

The holothuroids were too soft-bodied to be common as fossils, though their minute spicules sometimes occur abundantly in the Middle Palaeozoic rocks.

The echinoderm body

Before going on to describe first the holothuroids, a word or two about the general echinoderm body plan will not be out of place here. Most echinoderms are bilaterally symmetrical in their juvenile stages, but this is superseded in the adult by a five-branched radial arrangement. An alimentary canal constitutes the digestive system, but while a mouth is invariably present, there may or may not be an anus. The mouth is usually central, but the anus may be situated on the opposite side of the body, or on the same side. There is a system of water canals known as the *water vascular system*, and a radiating nerve-system, and the ectoderm is characteristically strengthened by the deposition within its tissues of carbonate of lime in the form of spicules or other components.

The water canals referred to above are one of the most characteristic as well as the most constant of all echinoderm body features. This system consists of a series of membranous tubes filled with an aqueous fluid, apparently serving a respiratory function. There is a main circular canal surrounding the entrance to the alimentary tract, from which secondary canals radiate. These radial canals support numerous short lateral tubes, from which branched external processes resembling gills arise.

In the echinoderms the sexes are usually distinct, the reproductive organs being located in the coelom except in the crinoids, in which they are found in the tentacles.

Echinoderms secrete carbonate of lime in their outer integument, which has, of course, facilitated the preservation of most groups as fossils. The actual plan of the echinoderm exoskeleton is so characteristic that even the smallest fragment can usually be recognised with certainty under the microscope. In the first place, the calcareous tissue has a very characteristic crystalline structure; the skeleton of fossil forms, owing to mineralisation, exhibits, even in fragments of microscopic size, the unmistakable rhombohedral cleavage of calcite. Even in specimens whose reticulated skeletal structure has been partly obliterated by metamorphic earth-activity subsequent to fossilisation, this characteristic cleavage still remains. The persistence of this microstructure is of inestimable assistance to the palaeontologist, enabling him to identify echinoderm remains with absolute certainty even from microscopic fragments of indeterminate shape (see Fig. 20).

Secondly, the organic structure of the skeleton itself is based on a constant principle of series of reticulated calcareous rods; all echinoderms exhibit this network in their skeletal structure, the various groups differing merely in the size and disposition of the meshes.

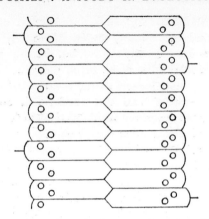

FIG. 20   Microscopic section of calcareous tissue in echinoids, showing
typical cleavage (× 60)

The holothuroids

The body form of holothuroids is slug-like, the mouth being at the anterior extremity and the anus at the opposite end. Unlike other echinoderms, the members of this group have very restricted powers of calcification of their tissues, this being limited to a few sporadically-distributed spicules, mostly of microscopic size, which may be globular, wheel-shaped, anchor-shaped, hooked at one end, or of other forms. Under microscopic examination these spicules, whatever their shape, exhibit the unmistakable netted structure referred to earlier.

The geological history of the holothuroids is very imperfectly known, the oldest authenticated remains having been found in the Carboniferous rocks of Scotland, although remains of animals thought to belong to the group have been collected from Ordovician rocks. A few others have been discovered in Jurassic, Middle Eocene and Pliocene deposits on the continent of Europe, and in post-Tertiary deposits in Bute.

The cystoids

We shall now briefly discuss the first of the two extinct groups.

The cystoids are mainly pedunculate (stalked) and in life were attached to the ocean floor. In this particular they resembled the crinoids, but here the similarity ends, as while the crinoids have feathery 'arms' or tentacles, the cystoids are either quite devoid of these appendages, or the latter are very imperfectly developed. The shape of the animal varies from globular or ovate to pear-shaped or conical, and this head-like structure (which is really the animal's body as, of course, it has no 'head' as we understand the term) is called the *calyx*, the 'stalk' usually being referred to as the *column*. In a few species this column was truncated or even absent and the animal was sessile, being attached to the substratum by the base of the calyx.

The calyx is covered by a number of polygonal plates, usually irregular in disposition. An aperture functioning as a mouth appears at the surface of the calyx opposite the point of its attachment to the column (or substratum, in the case of the sessile species), and a second orifice, the anus, is situated at any point elsewhere on the upper surface of the calyx, according to species. In some specimens a minute third opening may be discerned near the mouth; this is the *genital pore*, from which reproductive elements were released to the exterior.

In well-preserved examples the upper surface of the calyx exhibits grooves radiating from the mouth: these are termed the *food grooves* and doubtless served to direct currents of water containing food over the surface of the body and into the mouth.

Cystoids are confined entirely to the Palaeozoic period, their remains having been found in deposits ranging from the Cambrian to the Carboniferous. Their peak of development was attained during the Ordovician. Around Llandeilo and Bala in North Wales cystoid remains are abundant in the Ordovician strata. They became less common in the Silurian, and only a very few forms are known from the Devonian rocks; in the Carboniferous deposits only one genus has so far been discovered.

The blastoids

The blastoids differ from the cystoids in that the calyx exhibits complete radial symmetry and is enclosed by calcareous plates arranged in a definite pattern (see Fig. 21). A column is usually, though not always, present. The five petaloid radials give the body a distinctive bud-like appearance, from which the group takes its name (Gr. *blastos*, bud, and *eidos*, form). Food-grooves are

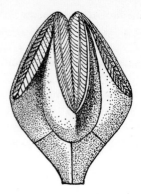

FIG. 21   Calyx of *Pentatremites pyriformis* ($\times 1\frac{1}{2}$)

present, as in cystoids, but 'arms' or tentacles are never developed.

The most remarkable structures in the blastoids are the respiratory tubes or *hydrospires,* which do not occur in other groups. Each hydrospire consists of a flattened lamellar tube with thin calcareous walls, extensively involuted, and dilated at their distal extremities. Water enters these tubes through slit-like apertures on their external surfaces, and at their distal ends a group of either five or ten openings (according to species) served to facilitate the expulsion of water.

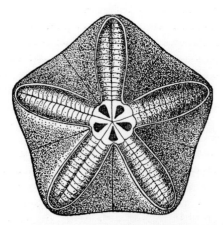

FIG. 22   *Pentatremites cervinus,* dorsal view (after Hall) ($\times 1\frac{1}{2}$)

Blastoid remains have not been unearthed from deposits earlier than the Ordovician. A few forms have turned up in the Silurian rocks of North America, and in the Devonian deposits both in the Old and the New World various genera are represented. Carboniferous times, however, saw the maximum development of the group, the type genus *Pentatremites* (Fig. 22) occurring here here for the first time. Above the horizon of the Carboniferous Limestone no blastoids have as yet been discovered.

The asteroids or starfishes

The asteroids of ancient times looked very much like modern starfishes, and can be briefly described as echinoderms with five *rays*, or 'arms', arranged in the familiar star-like shape, the central portion or *disc* being the 'body' proper. The rays are hollow and contain extensions of the viscera. The outer integument is coriaceous and is strengthened by irregularly-disposed calcareous plates, or in some cases is studded with calcareous spines. The mouth, which is centrally-situated, is on the lower surface of the disc. In many cases it serves also for the excretion of wastes, no separate anus being present; but in a few species there is a dorsal anus. Starfishes move by means of *ambulacral tube-feet,* which are extruded from grooves on the under-surface of the rays.

Some starfishes, both ancient and modern, differ markedly in form from the more common type in which the 'arms' form free extensions of the body, such as the Ordovician *Palaeaster niagarensis* (Fig. 23), but even in those species in which the rays do not form free extensions they are nevertheless still plainly discernible, extending from the middle of the disc to the five points of the pentagon which forms the periphery of the body. An example of this type is *Goniaster,* which is shown at Fig. 24. However, this type of body conformation among starfishes is in the minority, and in fact the length of the rays is one of the most variable features of the group; in the vast majority of both living and extinct forms the disc is inconspicuous.

An interesting structure found on the dorsal surface of the disc, usually at the angle of junction of two of the rays, is the *madreporite,* a tiny aperture covered by a calcareous plate, whose function appears to be to protect the water-vascular system from injury. The mouth is similarly protected by calcareous plates, the *oral plates,* arranged in five pairs. Deep furrows, known as the *ambulacral grooves,* radiate

C

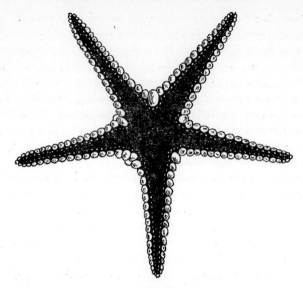

FIG. 23   *Palaeaster niagarensis* (× 3)

from the mouth, one along the underside of each arm, from which arise rows of suctorial *tube-feet*.

The exoskeleton of starfishes is less highly-developed than in the next group we shall be considering (the echinoids or sea-urchins) after the starfishes and brittle-stars. In the starfishes the outer integument consists of numerous small calcareous ossicles, loosely linked together. This 'chain-mail armour' is typically reticulated in appearance, the interstices being filled by the coriaceous ectoderm. (This may be very well observed in *Goniaster*, shown at Fig. 24).

The water-vascular system of the asteroids, called the *ambulacral system,* opens to the exterior between two of the rays, this opening being protected by the madreporite already referred to. The madreporite admits water to a short canal which opens into the circular vessel surrounding the gullet. From this circular canal arise five *ambulacral vessels,* running longitudinally along the under-surface of the rays, which also bear radiating nerve-cords. There may be two or four rows of tube-feet arising from each ambulacral groove.

The main difference between the starfishes and the sea-urchins is that the radiating ambulacral vessels in starfishes are situated externally, while in the sea-urchins these structures are covered over by a calcified integument; more will be said about this in the section on echinoids.

However, the radiating ambulacral vessels of starfishes are not entirely vulnerable: they are protected by an internal calcareous 'skeleton', which is not present in the sea-urchins. This so-called 'skeleton' is really a series of two rows of elongated calcareous plates forming a roof-shaped structure over the ambulacral groove on the underside of each ray.

In addition to the ambulacral vessels, starfishes possess a system of respiratory organs known as the *dermal branchiae*. These are delicate extensions of the ectoderm and are directly connected with the central body cavity. In some orders, such as the *Cryptogonia*, these dermal branchiae are distributed all over the body, while in one recent order, the *Phanerogonia*, they are restricted to the dorsal surface only.

The reproductive bodies in asteroids are discharged from minute sieve-like openings in the angles between the rays. While these apertures can be seen under microscopic examination in living forms,

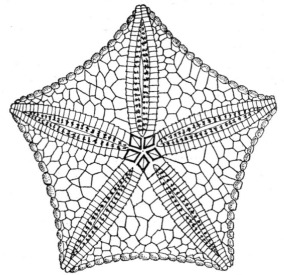

FIG. 24   *Goniaster* (× 3)

they are too minute to admit of recognition in fossilised specimens.

Living asteroids are principally denizens of littoral and rock-pool habitats, but some types live submerged in shallow waters, while a few forms are found even at great depths. The starfishes are a group of great antiquity, the earliest authenticated members of the class having been discovered in the Ordovician rocks, but certain fossil echinoderms from the Upper Cambrian are thought by some authorities to be early asteroids.

Starfishes may be classified into two main sub-groups, one of which, the *Euasteroidea,* is the only type now in existence. In this group the two rows of ambulacral ossicles which form the 'roof' over each ambulacral groove are placed opposite each other. The fossil forms of this group are found principally in the later strata, especially those of Tertiary origin; while members of the other sub-group, the *Encrinasteriae,* do not appear to have survived since Palaeozoic times. This group is characterised by the two rows of ambulacral ossicles being so placed as to alternate with each other.

The ophiuroids or brittle-stars

The ophiuroids or brittle-stars may be immediately differentiated as a class from the starfishes by having greatly-elongated 'arms'; in addition to this obvious feature, the rays do not contain diverticula from the alimentary tract, and are devoid of open ambulacral grooves on their ventral surfaces.

The central disc is pentagonal, as in starfishes, and the arms are both prehensile and locomotory. The ambulacral vessels, with their accompanying nerve-cords, are covered by a coriaceous or plated integument. The mouth is situated in the centre of the underside of the disc, and there is no anus, wastes being excreted via the buccal orifice. A pair of longitudinal fissure-like openings situated at the base of each of the five arms are the apertures from which the products of the gonads are released to the exterior.

The upper surface of the disc in ophiuroids is completely encrusted by calcareous plates, there being usually one larger *central plate* and a pair of *radial shields* at each of the points where the rays join the body. The ventral surface is similarly armoured, the largest plates surrounding the mouth; these are five in number and are known as the *mouth-shields.*

The arms are protected by four rows of calcareous plates, one dorsal, one ventral and two lateral; the latter carry rows of spines. Each ventral plate is so related to its corresponding laterals that a pair of apertures is formed on each side, through which the tube-feet are extruded.

In addition to a calcareous exoskeleton, ophiuroids also have an internal supporting system known as the *ambulacral skeleton,* consisting of a series of large calcareous discoid ossicles, known rather mis-leadingly as the *vertebral ossicles,* which occupy the greater part of the interior of each arm, and are grooved ventrally for the reception of the ambulacral vessel and radial nerve-cord. The entire structure articulates and is also supplied with muscles.

The marine deposits of almost all the great geological periods have yielded examples of this group, the oldest known forms occurring in Ordovician strata. Ophiuroids are, however, less common as fossils than many other echinoderms, and owing to the slenderness of the 'arms' they are exceedingly fragile, so it is little to be wondered at that nearly all the ophiuroid fossils that do turn up are imperfect specimens, and a complete and unspoiled fossil ophiuroid is exceedingly rare.

The echinoids or sea-urchins

The members of this class are characterised by the possession of a globular, spherical, heart-shaped, discoidal or depressed body, encased in a hard shell known as the *test,* which is composed of numerous rigidly-connected calcareous plates. There is a mouth and an anus; the former is always situated on the lower surface, but the position of the latter may vary. The intestinal tract is highly convoluted.

The ambulacral system in echinoids consists of an *oesophageal ring* from which five *radial vessels* arise. Five radial areas, corresponding with the five rays in starfishes and brittle-stars, are clearly discernible on the exterior of the test, following the direction of the five ambu-lacral vessels. The *tube-feet* are extruded from perforations in the calcareous plates of the test along these five radial areas, the inter-radial regions between them being imperforate. The external opening of the ambulacral system is closed by a calcareous plate, the *madreporite,* situated at the apex of the test in one of these inter-radial areas.

Since it is the hard test which has been preserved in fossil echinoids, it is this structure whose details must be studied by the palaeontologist if he is to identify the species occurring in any given strata. The test is essentially composed of the *corona*, which forms the main part, and the *apical disc*, which consists of a single or double row of plates at the summit of the corona.

The corona is composed of numerous calcareous plates, united firmly at their edges to form a rigid box-like structure protecting the soft body within. The first circle of coronal plates develops round the mouth, and the vertical growth of the test is effected by the calcification of successive rows of plates between those already formed and the apical disc.

The corona has five radial zones with five interradial areas, the latter being imperforate, while the former are arranged in such a way that minute pores are formed for the extrusion of tube-feet, these pores being usually paired.

In many echinoids the tube-feet can be extruded along the entire length of the radial zones; these are referred to as '*ambulacra perfecta*'. In some other sea-urchins, however, these areas are not continuously perforated, only their upper portions being uninterruptedly poriferous; such types are known as '*ambulacra circumscripta*' or *petaloid*. On this basis echinoids are sub-divided into two main groups.

The most important external structures to be seen on the surface of the corona are the *spines*, which are set into rounded excrescences, the *tubercles*. These vary a great deal according to family or genus both as to size and situation on the test.

The spines are movable appendages, jointed to the tubercles on the ball-and-socket principle. They are used defensively as well as in locomotion, and vary a great deal in length and shape.

Another sub-division of the group is based on the disposition of the plates constituting the apical disc. In typical or 'regular' forms this ring of plates surrounds the anus, while in the so-called 'irregular echinoids' the apical disc still occupies the summit of the test but the anus is eccentric, its position bearing no relation to the apical disc.

In those echinoids whose apical disc consists of a double row of plates, each of the five pentagonal plates constituting the inner row is perforated by the duct of a testis or ovary, and so these plates are known as the *genital plates*. One of these genital plates is larger than the other four and supports a tubercle perforated by many minute

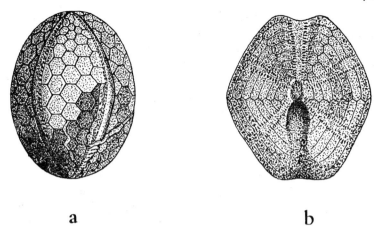

a   **b**

FIG. 25 (a) *Palaechinus ellipticus*, a regular echinoid, (b) *Hyboclypus gibberulus*, an irregular echinoid (× 1)

apertures; this is known as the *madreporiform tubercle*, the plate supporting it being termed the *madreporite*. The genital plates are always situated interradially.

Fossil echinoids range from the Ordovician to the Cenozoic, the maximum development of the class having occurred in the Cretaceous. Typical 'regular' and 'irregular' echinoids are shown at Fig. 25.

The crinoids or sea-lilies

We come now to the most interesting of all the fossil echinoderms, the crinoids or sea-lilies, which may be defined as echinoderms in which the body is fixed to the sea floor, either throughout life or during the juvenile stages only, by means of a jointed flexible 'stalk' or *peduncle*. The body is cup-shaped or discoidal and is protected dorsally by a series of calcareous plates. The mouth is situated on the upper surface, usually centrally, and from around it arise jointed flexible tentacle-like 'arms', which may vary in number but are always in multiples of five. They carry lateral jointed processes known as *pinnules*, and their ventral surfaces are furnished with grooves corresponding to the ambulacral grooves found in other echinoderms. The reproductive organs are situated below the surface of the ectoderm in these grooves.

All known crinoids are attached to a substratum in their young stages, but in the adult state they may either remain fixed or become free-swimming. On this basis the class is divided into two main sub-groups, the pedunculate crinoids and the free crinoids. A free crinoid such as *Comatula rosacea* (Fig. 26) bears a superficial resemblance to an ophiuroid when viewed dorsally, but a good many physiological differences become apparent on closer examination.

In the crinoids the 'apical disc' of the echinoids is replaced by a system of calcareous plates forming a cup-shaped *calyx*. The ventral surface of the body is covered by a coriaceous, sometimes partly-calcified, ectoderm, and carries the buccal orifice, which is normally central, but in one genus *(Actinometra)* it is eccentric. The anus is usually situated at the end of a short tubular projection, positioned eccentrically.

Along the ventral surfaces of the arms run the *ambulacral grooves*. The floor of the groove is ciliated, and below each runs a radiating

FIG. 26   *Comatula rosacea,* a free crinoid (× $\frac{4}{5}$)

water-vessel together with a nerve-cord. In the centre of each arm, between the calcareous skeleton and the water-vessel, are three tubular extensions of the body-cavity. The middle one, which is the largest, contains the gonads, while the other two circulate water from the body cavity.

The ciliated grooves continue from the proximal ends of the arms over the upper surface of the disc to the mouth, their function being to convey food carried in water-currents into the buccal orifice. The mouth opens into a spirally-coiled alimentary canal, which is contained wholly within the calyx; no diverticula extend from it into the arms.

The water-vascular system comprises a ring-like canal surrounding the mouth, with radiating water-vessels running along the ambulacral grooves. The circular canal communicates directly with the body cavity by numerous water-tubes, which distribute water admitted to the body cavity through minute pores in the body wall.

The nervous system is much more highly-developed in crinoids than in any other echinoderms. The nerve-cord which runs longitudinally beneath the floor of each ambulacral groove corresponds morphologically to the radiating nerve-cords in starfishes, but there are also some additional complex structures in crinoids, not found in other echinoderms, which zoologists have shown to be nervous in nature. A five-chambered central dorsal organ, enclosed in a fibrous sheath, gives rise in the pedunculate crinoids to five vessels which continue down the central canal of the column, and in both stalked and free crinoids a series of radial extensions, known as *axial cords,* arise from this central organ and occupy median canals within the skeleton of the arms, extending even into the pinnules, the muscles and the ectoderm. This type of nerve-system is not found in any other echinoderm group.

Basically the body plan of the stalked crinoids differs little from that of the free-living types, the structure of the ambulacral and vascular systems, the form and arrangement of the alimentary canal, and the nervous and reproductive systems being essentially similar in both. The majority of fossil crinoids belong to the pedunculate group. The stalk in transverse section is normally round, but in some genera, such as *Platycrinus,* it can be elliptical, while in others, such as *Extracrinus,* it is pentagonal.

The separate articulations of the column are so connected with one another that while the amount of movement between any two joints is somewhat limited, the entire column as a whole is much more flexible. In many forms the articulating facets are marked by more or less numerous radiating striae, which run from the central canal to the margin of each joint.

A very curious phenomenon may occasionally be observed, in which two adjacent stem-joints are united immovably by close ligamentous connection, subsequently producing more or less complete fusion, the original line of division usually remaining visible as a line of suture. This peculiar mode of union is known as *syzygy*.

The uppermost joint of the column adjacent to the calyx is usually larger than the inferior articulations, and is frequently differently-shaped. In some cases, e.g. the Jurassic *Apiocrinus,* from the Middle Oolites, the uppermost joint may actually enter into and form part of the conformation of the calyx. The most general method by which the height of the column is increased is by the growth of new joints at its summit.

The calyx is usually cup-shaped, and is entirely enclosed by a series of polygonal calcareous plates joined more or less closely together. In some types these plates are homogeneously united by firm sutures, while in others they are more or less movable and articulating. In still other forms certain of the plates may be connected by the peculiar mode of union already referred to as syzygy. In one rare genus, the Devonian *Hystricrinus,* the calycinal plates are furnished externally with movable articulating spines, somewhat resembling the prickly outer test of echinoids.

The crinoids of the Palaeozoic rocks differ in several respects from later forms from Secondary and Tertiary strata, which have been grouped together by one authority as the 'Neocrinoids'. Almost all these later crinoids resemble living forms in having open ambulacral grooves, whereas in Palaeozoic species only very rarely does the upper surface of the calyx exhibit open ambulacral grooves, nor is the mouth-opening normally exposed. The buccal orifice and the food-grooves in these species are normally completely concealed beneath a superficial covering of calcareous plates, the pattern of which varies according to family and genus. In several families, notably the *Actinocrinidae,* the *Platycrinidae* and the *Rhodocrinidae,* the ventral surface of the calyx is roofed over by a tectiform canopy of calcareous plates, which are firmly united with one another and completely conceal the ambulacral grooves and buccal orifice.

The reason why so many fossil crinoids of Palaeozoic origin *appear* to have open ambulacral grooves and a large mouth-opening is simply that these plates which covered them in life were so fragile that they were very easily destroyed, and in fact very few early crinoids are found with these delicate plates intact. The upper surface of the calyx then exhibits the grooves, together with their inter-radial zones and the mouth-opening, very clearly.

Classification of crinoids

Crinoids are sub-divided by most authorities into two main classes, the *Palaeocrinoidea* and the *Neocrinoidea*. The former class includes all those forms in which the arms are free of the calyx above their point of articulation with the radials; the latter class is characterised by forms whose calcyes 'grow up' ventrally and include some brachials within the actual cup. Each class is further sub-divided into various orders and sub-groups.

Palaeozoic crinoids (Palaeocrinoidea) usually have a massive and sometimes asymmetrical calyx which appears disproportionately large in comparison with the length of the arms. Mesozoic and Cenozoic forms (Neocrinoidea), on the other hand, are distinguished from the earlier forms by the comparatively small size and greater symmetry of the calyx and the greater proportionate length of the arms.

Relatively few living crinoids exist, as far as is known, compared with the abundance of their forbears. The free-living crinoids are all members of the family *Comatulidae*, represented by six genera comprising some 200 species; while of the stalked crinoids only about 40 living types are known, distributed among six genera. While the pedunculate crinoids are found only at great depths—from 2500 to 2900 fathoms—the free-swimming Comatulids are all inhabitants of shallow seas.

Throughout the whole of the Palaeozoic era the crinoids were the dominant echinoderms, and in fact many limestone deposits from the Ordovician to the Carboniferous are so extensively composed of the fragmentary remains of these organisms that they are referred to as crinoidal limestones. Plates 11 and 12 show outstanding examples of crinoids.

From Permian times onwards the Palaeocrinoids declined rapidly and were superseded by the Neocrinoids, which came in at the commencement of the Trias. Numerous new types appeared in the Jurassic and Cretaceous, but the crinoids by this time were already playing a less conspicuous part in echinoderm history.

The earliest forms of the modern family of the *Comatulidae* appeared in the Middle Lias. Since the Tertiary formations are not rich in crinoid remains, many authorities incline towards the view that the comparatively limited recent crinoid fauna represents a survival from the early Mesozoic, an opinion which seems to be borne out by the fact that most living types closely resemble forms which existed when the Triassic and Jurassic systems were laid down.

6

Jamoytius—Forerunner of Amphioxus?

WHILE most authorities seem to be in agreement that the lowly amphioxus is the most primitive chordate relative of the vertebrates, its origin is shrouded in obscurity and several hypothetical conclusions have been drawn in various quarters, none of which, while claiming some plausible explanation, can be definitely substantiated by irrefutable evidence sufficiently to be universally accepted as fact. Consequently, while the various fossil forms purporting to be the ancient ancestors of amphioxus may all have played some part in its evolutionary development, none can be categorically stated to be *the* 'missing link' (if I may be pardoned for using this much-abused term).

In this chapter we shall explore the possibilities offered by the Upper Silurian *Jamoytius,* whose chief claim to the title lies in its almost identical physiological form. This, on the other hand, is offset by the fact that after *Jamoytius* became extinct no other similar organism appeared until the actual first occurrence of amphioxus in modern times. While one could, of course, draw the obvious inference that intermediate forms did in fact exist but have remained undiscovered, many authorities, understandably, find it hard to comprehend why no such intermediate forms have turned up in strata from the intervening geological eras. This is certainly one of the mysteries of the palaeontologist's world, which we can only hope may be solved in the not-too-distant future. After all, coelacanths were thought to have become extinct 70 million years ago until one turned up in 1938, virtually unchanged. That is a story which we shall be discussing in a later chapter, and it is quite the most exciting discovery of the modern scientific world—but I here refer to it as a somewhat analogous situation.

Getting back to our original query, let us now compare amphioxus with *Jamoytius* and see what morphological similarities link these two lowly organisms, at the same time noting any points of divergence which may help to throw some light on the mysterious time-lag between the apparent demise of *Jamoytius* and the advent of its modern successor.

The word *amphioxus* means 'pointed at both ends', which aptly describes the shape of both this animal and *Jamoytius,* first discovered in the Upper Silurian estuarine shale of Scotland. Its torpedo-shaped body, only a few inches long, displays both median and lateral fin folds, and the head bears a pair of large eyes; in these particulars it differs from amphioxus. In most other respects, however, it closely resembles its more recent counterpart, which is also an inhabitant of coastal and estuarine waters.

Physiologically we know, of course, much more about amphioxus than *Jamoytius,* since only the harder parts of the latter have been preserved, together with some impressions left in the solidified mud. Amphioxus is about two inches or so in length, and despite its streamlined shape adapted for fast swimming, it spends much of its time buried up to the neck (a term I conveniently use here in a metaphorical rather than a biological sense) in the sand or mud of the shore or bottom. It has a notochord, a dorsal nerve-cord and gills, and is furnished also with a simple digestive tract situated ventrally—all of the foregoing being, as we have already seen, typical vertebrate characteristics.

A pigment spot at the anterior end of the body appears to be light-sensitive; at this juncture it is interesting to compare *Jamoytius* with its paired eyes. This suggests that *Jamoytius* was much more active as a swimming predator, while amphioxus, content to lie almost completely buried and wait for prey to drift on the current within reach of the ciliated mouthparts, has little need of visual powers and so eyes have become superfluous. Another small pit would appear to function as a rudimentary nostril.

Whereas a typical vertebrate (or vertebrate embryo) has only five or six pairs of gill-slits, amphioxus has about 60 pairs. It is a feature of the lower animals that the more typically primitive characteristics are emphasised, which is what appears to have happened here; in fact as the amphioxus grows, the gill-slits increase in number (another characteristically primitive feature). In this and certain other aspects amphioxus would seem, therefore, at first sight to be far less advanced than its kinsman of those far-off Upper Silurian times; but one could quite plausibly say that amphioxus has become more specialised for a half-buried existence, and thus needed to develop more gill-slits to enable it to absorb more oxygen from its somewhat limited environment, which *Jamoytius* did not need to do if it was an active swimmer. Similarly, one could take the line that, while eyes were essential to an active predator like *Jamoytius*, the lack of eyes was little handicap to amphioxus, so they have gradually degenerated. We shall probably never know the true solution to this puzzle.

7

Armoured for Survival

The ostracoderms or jawless fishes

FROM the Upper Silurian to the Devonian, aptly named the Age of Fishes, was but a step in the geological time-scale; but it was this step that was to prove the most vital step of all, the turning-point in evolutionary history, which saw the first vertebrates firmly established. Where, as the Upper Silurian period was drawing to a close, only *Jamoytius* held the fort, as it were, for the chordates, foreshadowing the coming of the vertebrates, by the commencement of Devonian times the waters were peopled with the first true backboned animals.

These, the most ancient predecessors of man, were as strange as the world in which they lived. Although sufficiently fish-like in form to justify classifying them as fishes, they were utterly unlike any fishes living to-day. Besides being heavily scaled from head to tail, the head and opercular regions were encased in a massive bony armour, which has prompted the adoption of the term *ostracoderms* ('shell-skinned') for this group. Despite their unwieldy, top-heavy appearance, on closer scrutiny it will be observed that these creatures have so many structural similarities to the living lampreys and hagfishes that a true relationship is apparent. Like the lampreys, the ostracoderms had but a single nostril situated high up on the head, no true jaws, and no paired fins; but it is when we come to examine the structure of the skull in detail that we can at once see the affinities between the two groups.

Both ostracoderms and lampreys represent the most primitive stage of vertebrate evolution. However, for various reasons which we have not space to enter into here, palaeontologists consider that the ostracoderms were a side-line, as it were, from the main stem of fishy evolution—a theory which is borne out by the fact that the group flourished for a short time and then died out quite suddenly, while the lampreys and hagfishes persist up to the present day. The most recent researches seem to show that the armoured fishes were probably exceedingly close to the line of descent of both lampreys and the higher fishes which followed later.

Bone, whether in the form of an internal skeleton or external armour-plating, is one of the most fundamental vertebrate characteristics. Why did these fishes need the protection of huge bony plates? Obviously for protection from their enemies; but what enemies could have been predators of such a well-protected group?

The fossil record shows that a very conspicuous invertebrate group, the eurypterids or water-scorpions, which belonged to the class Arachnida, were contemporaneous with and inhabited the same situations as the ostracoderms. While the latter were seldom more than a foot in length, the eurypterids were anything up to 12 feet long, and from the structure of their mouthparts were obviously carnivorous, with massive, powerful chelicerae which would make short work of even the most heavily-armoured of the little ostracoderms. Skeletons of the two groups are almost invariably found together in the same deposits.

Let us now look briefly at some of the ostracoderms which, together with the *Petromyzontidae* (lampreys) and the *Myxinidae* (hagfishes) make up the class *Agnatha* ('without jaws'). The ostracoderms are sub-divided into two sub-orders, as follows:

Class *Agnatha*

(1) *Pteraspida* (without a dorsal nostril)
(2) *Cephalaspida* (with a dorsal nostril)

The Pteraspida—the first true vertebrates
The first group, the *Pteraspida,* are the earliest known true vertebrates. From the Upper Silurian the group continued into the Upper Devonian, but it was in the Lower Devonian that it reached the peak of its development. Rather under a foot in length, members of the group are characterised by having a bony exoskeleton without enclosed bone-cells, forming an armour-like protective covering to the anterior part of the body. This covering consists of three distinct layers: an outer layer of dentine, a median layer of vascular bone, and an inner laminated layer. The outer layer in most species consists of a series of greatly elongated placoid scales or denticles, similar to those of modern dogfishes.

The mouth is normally ventral, but in one type, *Drepanaspis,* it is situated dorsally. From the disposition of the plates around the mouth it would seem that during life there must have been a suctorial or shovelling apparatus capable of extrusion, as the animals were bottom-feeders.

The branchial pouches are enclosed in a *cephalic shield,* and open to the exterior by pores, as in the modern hagfishes, the external gill-openings being covered by elongated branchial plates. There is no nasal orifice, this feature, or rather the lack of it, being the main point of difference serving to distinguish pteraspids from the other main sub-group, the cephalaspids. The neurocranium is never ossified, but from impressions left on the inner side of the dorsal shield it would appear that there are only two semicircular canals, and seven branchial pouches.

The lateral line system is well-developed, and its detailed arrangement is almost identical with the same structures in the modern lamprey *(Petromyzon).*

The anterior part of the body is somewhat flattened dorso-ventrally, the posterior part being laterally compressed. There are no paired fins, neither is there a dorsal or an anal fin. The tail fin is hypocercal, the ventral lobe being the larger—a modification for bottom-dwelling in a fish devoid of pectoral fins.

Within the order *Pteraspida* there is a general evolutionary trend from the earlier forms with the cephalic shield composed of only a few plates to the later species in which there are many. In the Upper Silurian *Poraspis heintzi* (Fig. 27), for example, the cephalic shield is divided into only a few plates, while in the Lower Devonian *Pteraspis rostrata* (Fig. 28) it will be seen that the plates which make up the armour of the head are more numerous. In the earlier forms these plates did not increase in size once they had been formed,

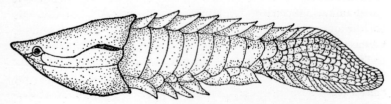

FIG. 27   *Poraspis heintzi* (after Heintz) ($\times 1\frac{1}{3}$)

which suggests a long-protracted larval or juvenile stage and late metamorphosis.

The Cephalaspida

The *Cephalaspida* range from the Upper Silurian to the end of the Devonian and are anatomically the best-known of all ostracoderms, the internal structure of the head being known in great detail. The famous palaeontologist Stensiö, during the course of researches carried out in the early part of the present century, found that, since all the connective tissue of the head in cephalaspids was ossified and all the foramina lined with perichondral bone, it was possible to describe in minute detail the shape and extent of the brain, and the courses taken by the various cranial nerves, in a way previously undreamt of in fossil fishes. A typical restoration is

FIG. 28   *Pteraspis rostrata* (after White) ($\times \frac{1}{3}$)

shown at Fig. 29, the example taken being *Kiaeraspis auchenaspidoides*.

The cephalaspids are usually rather small fishes, with the notable exception of the Middle Devonian *Cephalaspis magnifica,* which reached a length of 2 feet. There is an *undivided* bony head-shield extending some distance along the body. The head is compressed dorso-ventrally, but the body becomes progressively more and more laterally compressed towards its posterior end.

The exoskeleton differs from that of the *Pteraspida* in that the median and inner layers contain enclosed bone-cells. The denticles of the outer layer in cephalaspids also tend to be less distinctly discernible.

The mouth is ventral, the animals having been bottom-feeders. The orbits are situated dorsally, close together and separated by the *pineal foramen,* immediately anterior to which lies a median nostril, a feature which at once distinguishes cephalaspids from the preced-

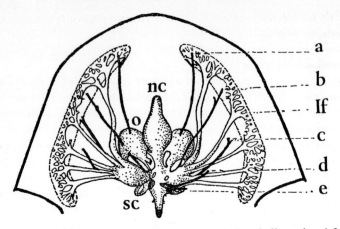

Fig. 29 *Kiaeraspis auchenaspidoides:* restoration of cephalic region (after Stensiö). Nerves shown by black lines: (a) profundus nerve, (b) trigeminal nerve, (c) facial nerve, (d) glossopharyngeal nerve, (e) vagus nerve, (lf) lateral electric field, (nc) nasal capsule, (sc) semicircular canal, (o) orbit

ing group. The conformation of the skull is almost identical with that of the living lamprey.

The head-shield, which is comparatively small, forms a continuous plate enclosing the brain. Stensiö considered that certain areas served by several large nerves may have supported electric fields (see Fig. 29 already referred to supra).

There are nine or ten pairs of gill-slits, and the shape of the gill-pouches is the same as in modern agnathous fishes. A remarkable feature is the presence of an additional anterior gill-slit in front of the hyoid—a condition unknown in any other vertebrate group.

The brain closely resembles that of *Petromyzon,* particularly in the shape of the olfactory lobes, but the bilobate cerebellum is more reminiscent of the hagfishes. The auditory capsules are proportionately large, but there are only two semicircular canals, the horizontal one being absent, as in modern agnathids. The cranial nerves are to all intents and purposes identical with analogous structures in *Petromyzon,* with the exception of the modification in the modern lamprey of the division of the trigeminal nerve into mandibular and maxillary branches, which is clearly a specialisation.

The lateral line system is much less easily discernible in cephalaspids, as it is not embedded in the bony exoskeleton but merely leaves a series of frequently-interrupted superficial grooves to indicate its course.

In some genera, such as the Upper Silurian *Aceraspis,* there are two dorsal fins, but in the majority of forms there is only one, the anterior being represented by a row of dorsal scutes. The caudal fin is heterocercal. Paired pectoral fins are present in most forms, and the pelvic fins appear to be represented only by ventro-lateral ridges.

With the passage of time the predaceous eurypterids, arch-enemies of the ostracoderms, became extinct, and the primitive vertebrates did not need this external bony armour. As this tended to become reduced, more progressive features began to supersede it, such as a streamlined shape to facilitate fast swimming, and an increase in size. The most important step forward, however, was the development of jaws. Only by developing adequate gnathic structures could vertebrates become active predators, no longer restricted to a mud-grubbing and bottom-dwelling existence. For the pursuit of prey faster movement was essential, and this led to the evolution of paired fins which, together with the more streamlined form of the body, enabled the fishes eventually to dominate the waters.

8

The Age of Fishes—I

The origin of jaws

IN ORDER to understand how vertebrate jaws developed, the structures from which they originated are most easily seen from a study of the cranial skeleton of fishes of the shark group, or *Chondrichthyes*. This word means 'cartilaginous fishes'; in other words, fishes whose skeleton is not composed of bone but of cartilage or gristle. Although jaw modifications may be easily observed in a modern shark or dog-fish, these are nowhere more obvious than in the Devonian shark *Cladoselache* (see Chapter 9).

Taking *Cladoselache* as our model, we shall discover that the gill bars which lie between the gill openings are divided into upper and lower branches; the jaws are situated in line with these and are similarly composed of upper and lower parts, the upper being known as the *palatoquadrate* and the lower as *Meckel's cartilage*. It seems apparent that the first true jaws must have been merely a modification of the first pair of these gill bars, which had developed a new function during the course of evolution (see Fig. 30). The origin of teeth may similarly be traced from the denticles, small pointed structures found in the skin in primitive fishes, which are almost similar to teeth in structure.

The Placoderms

The oldest known jawed vertebrates, primitive ancestors of the higher fishes, did not appear until the end of the Silurian and the beginning of the Devonian. At this time ostracoderms were still abundant and, like them, the early jawed fishes were heavily armoured. Jaws were still in the experimental stage and their mode of suspension was as yet of the most primitive type, known as *aphetohyoid* ('free hyoid'), in which the hyomandibular arch is not fused along its entire length to the upper jaw.

The placoderms, or *Aphetohyoidea*, consist of six main groups, as follows:

Class *Placodermi* (Aphetohyoidea)

(1) Acanthodii—the so-called 'spiny sharks'
(2) Arthrodira—'jointed-necked' fishes
(3) Macropetalichthyida—armoured forms related to the above
(4) Antiarchi—small armoured species with movable jointed pectoral spines
(5) Stegoselachii—flattened, skate-like forms
(6) Palaeospondyloidea—one species, *Palaeospondylus problematicus*

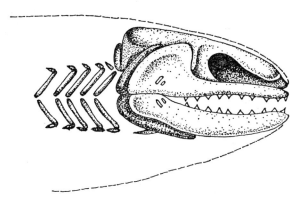

Fig. 30   Development of jaws from gill-arches in *Cladoselache*

The Acanthodians

Typical of these early jawed fishes were the *acanthodians*, often misleadingly called 'the spiny sharks'. These river-dwellers, which, of course, were not sharks at all, were covered with bony plates, and their most important feature was the development of *paired fins*, attached to the pectoral and pelvic girdles in the same way as our own limbs. The pattern was already being laid for the coming of the higher vertebrates.

The acanthodians enjoyed the longest run of all placoderms, ranging from the Upper Silurian to the Lower Permian. They are usually fishes of small size, with a few exceptions reaching 2 feet. The

FIG. 31   *Climatius* (much reduced)

body is fusiform in shape (giving rise, no doubt, to the 'shark' association) and either one or two dorsal fins may be present. There is an anal fin and a heterocercal caudal fin, and in addition to the paired pectoral and pelvic fins there is a series of intermediate fin-spines, which are of particular interest as they appear to support the view that paired fins were originally continuous lateral folds of the body wall. All the fins except the caudal are supported by an anterior fin-spine which, in primitive forms such as the Lower Devonian *Climatius* (Fig. 31), is restricted to the skin, this spine being little more than an enlarged scale. In later forms such as *Acanthodes* (Fig. 32), from the Carboniferous and Permian, the spines are laterally flattened, but their bases arise from between the myotomes, a considerable distance inside the body.

The acanthodian body is covered with a characteristic arrangement of small lozenge-shaped ganoid scales, made up of concentric layers of bone penetrated by minute branching canals from the

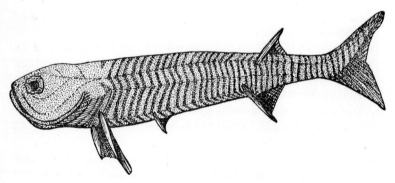

FIG. 32   *Acanthodes* (much reduced)

exterior. The outer layers are glossy and transparent, resembling the ganoine of the scales of Actinopterygians (q.v.).

The nostrils are small, situated close together in the middle line. The eyes are large and are placed far forward, and are surrounded by a few bony plates. The neurocranium is well-known only in the type genus, *Acanthodes*; in general shape it is rather like that of actinopterygians, with an attenuated occipital region, the brain cavity being situated immediately above a narrow inter-orbital septum. The palatoquadrate and Meckel's cartilage may be either ossified into a single unit, as in *Climatius,* or the palatoquadrate may be divided into three integral component parts and Meckel's cartilage into two distinct sections, as in *Acanthodes.* Teeth, when present, are either simple and conical in form, or may be compressed laterally with a prominent median cusp and one or two lateral cusps on either side, as in *Climatius.*

The Arthrodira

We come now to the *Arthrodira* or 'jointed-necked' fishes, which are a very extensive group ranging in time from the Lower to the Upper Devonian. They were essentially predators, some of them reaching a very formidable size; the most well-known, *Dinichthys,* was a huge, ferocious-looking creature 26 to 30 feet in length! Resemblances in the structure of the neurocranium, together with similarities in the dermal girdles, fin-spines, mode of jaw-suspension and the presence of a mandibular operculum clearly indicate a close relationship between the Arthrodira and the Acanthodii.

The jointed-necked fishes always have a cephalic shield articulating with a thoracic carapace, both of which are formed of a number of bony plates containing bone-cells. Posteriorly the body tapers, and the tail was probably heterocercal. The posterior region of the body is usually found devoid of any dermal covering, but in a few forms imbricating cycloid scales have been described.

The pectoral fin is represented by a spine, either immovably fixed to the thoracic carapace, or articulating with it. A gap on the pectoral armour behind this spine points to the probability that there may also have been a small pectoral fin; moreover, in some forms a few radials have been discovered behind the pectoral spine. The pelvic girdle is formed from two component parts, and there is a pelvic fin supported by a few radials. Two rows of radials support the dorsal fin, and the presence of a large plate in the anal region suggests that there may have been an anal fin. There are usually no complete centra in the vertebral column, the notochord being unconstricted.

The eyes are large, laterally-situated and placed relatively far forward; the nostrils are small and lie anteriorly, close together in the middle line. The neurocranium, where known, is lined by perichondral bone. There is evidence that the teeth were arranged in more than one row, suggesting derivation from the acanthodian type of dentition, though in most specimens the original denticles have been superseded by biting plates of bone.

Macropetalichthys

This is the type genus of an order of placoderms ranging from the Lower to the Upper Devonian which in many ways resembles the Arthrodira. Dorso-ventrally flattened, they possess a cephalic shield and a pectoral carapace with immovable pectoral fin-spines. The lateral line system is well-marked, the tail diphycercal, and there are two dorsal fins or spines. These fishes, which never attained any great size, are very imperfectly known; the structure of the jaws and teeth remains yet to be discovered.

In *Macropetalichthys* the neurocranium is platybasic, with an attenuated occipital region. The entire structure is ossified into a single unit, and bears striking resemblances to that of both the Acanthodii and the Arthrodira. The nostrils lie close together in the middle line, and the nasal capsules must have been small.

The Antiarchi

These were highly-specialised placoderms which first appeared in the Middle Devonian but had already become extinct by the end of the Upper Devonian. The group, which consists of relatively small fishes under a foot in length, was for a long time considered to be related to the ostracoderms, but later studies have shown these fishes to be derived from an ancestral form of the jointed-necked fishes.

The head and anterior part of the body are covered with bony shields formed of imbricating plates containing bone-cells. These plates are arranged in a constant and characteristic manner. The posterior part of the body in the Middle Devonian *Pterichthyodes*

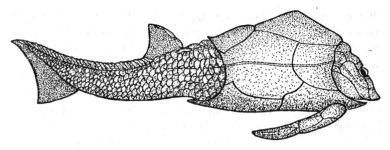

FIG. 33   *Pterichthyodes* (reduced)

(Fig. 33) is covered with overlapping cycloid scales, with a dorsal ridge, but in the Upper Devonian *Bothriolepis* (Fig. 34) the body is naked. In *Pterichthyodes* there is one dorsal fin; in *Bothriolepis* there are two. The tail is heterocercal, and there is no anal fin.

The cephalic shield is smaller than the thoracic, which bears an articulating spine-like pectoral fin. In all except one form this spine is jointed about half-way down; in another form, *Ceraspis* from the Middle Devonian, the pectoral carapace is elongated dorsally to form a spine.

The pelvic fins have been described only in *Bothriolepis,* in which they have obviously derived from folds of skin directly behind the pectoral carapace. The latter forms a massive box-like structure with a flattened base, consisting of a number of bones easily comparable with those of typical Arthrodira but differing in the presence of an anterior as well as a posterior median dorsal plate, which is not found in the Arthrodira.

The eyes of Antiarchi are situated close together in a depression,

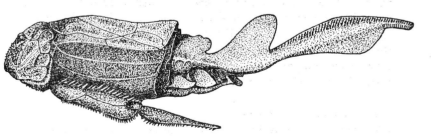

FIG. 34   *Bothriolepis* ($\times \frac{1}{3}$)

and between them lies a small plate, the *pineal plate,* bearing a foramen for the reception of the pineal. In front of this lies another small plate, the *pre-pineal,* which is notched at its anterior edge; these notches are interpreted by most authorities as nostrils.

The neurocranium in the Antiarchi is unknown, but the nasal capsules must have been small and close together. The mouth is ventral, bounded dorsally by the *maxillary plate* and ventrally by the *mandibular plate,* each of which has a denticulated biting edge.

The lateral line sensory canal system consists of two distinct series of open grooves, one series larger than the other.

The affinities of the Antiarchi with the Arthrodira are based primarily on similarities between the cephalic and pectoral shields in the two groups. The presence of an operculum and of groove-like sensory canals are further points of resemblance. It is generally agreed by the most recent authorities that the pectoral fins of Antiarchi are derived from bony spines such as those possessed by the jointed-necked fishes.

The Stegoselachii

Included in this order are a few Devonian fishes, the majority of which are very poorly-known. All have a *superficial* external resemblance to modern selachians—so much so, in fact, that many of the older authorities considered them to be closely related to the chondrichthyoid fishes.

However, on further study it will become apparent that such a relationship is only what one might term an 'optical illusion'. Firstly, all of them have an exoskeleton of dermal bony plates on the head and anterior part of the body; bone is never present in true chondrichthyoids, either inside or outside the body. Secondly, these fishes, which occur in the Lower Devonian, are already much more highly-advanced than even the earliest Upper Devonian chondrichthyoids. Thirdly, all the available evidence suggests that the *Stegoselachii* were all operculate fishes and that the hyomandibular played no part in their mode of jaw suspension—the opposite is true in cartilaginous fishes.

The Palaeospondyloidea

This group contains but a single species of the type genus *Palaeospondylus*; this species has been aptly named *problematicus* owing to its peculiarities which place it apart from all other placoderms.

The true affinities of this form have been shrouded in mystery ever since its discovery; it has at various times been accorded the status of an agnathid, a chondrichthyoid, a larval form of the Dipnoi, even the larval form of an amphibian. One authority even went so far as to suggest that it represented an altogether new class! However, the most recent research workers have decided, somewhat diffidently, that *Palaeospondylus problematicus* is actually a placoderm of highly-specialised form.

FIG. 35 *Palaeospondylus problematicus*

Palaeospondylus (Fig. 35) is a small fish, seldom exceeding 2 ins in length. The skull, vertebral column and caudal fin are well-developed and calcified. There are traces on the skeleton of paired fins, probably pelvic. The vertebral column is composed of well-formed ring-like centra, except in the caudal region, and the tail is heterocercal.

The neurocranium is compressed dorso-ventrally, but at least a part of the roof of the skull appears to have been uncalcified. The auditory capsules are large, and beneath the neurocranium lie several paired rods which are almost certainly branchial arches; anterior to them lie two structures which would appear to be the palatoquadrate and the lower jaw. If this is a correct assumption, then it would seem probable that the hyomandibular played no part in jaw suspension.

The theory that *Palaeospondylus* is a larval form has been abandoned largely because, while the neurocranium is in very much the same stage of development as the chondrocranium in many larval forms, the vertebral column is composed of fully-developed centra, and the smallest known specimens (about $\frac{1}{2}$ in.) are no different in this respect from the largest ones. The presence of a heterocercal tail, and the apparent likelihood of the aphetohyoidal mode of jaw suspension, support an overwhelming case for including this palaeontological puzzle in the Placodermi. *Palaeospondylus* differs, however, from all other known placoderms in being devoid of any exoskeleton.

9

The Age of Fishes—II

The adaptability of the cartilaginous body

MEANWHILE the chondrichthyoids or true sharks were now evolving and colonising the waters. They were still heavily outnumbered by the ostracoderms, possibly because they were not yet sufficiently well adapted to make the greatest possible use of the available food supply. When, much later, there occurred a vast migration of bony fishes into the seas, from that point onwards chondrichthyoid fishes progressed apace, the higher fishes, which greatly outnumbered them, becoming their main source of food. This balance still obtains at the present day.

Let us now look at some of these early sharks, whose teeth are plentiful as fossils in various deposits. This group of fishes is sub-divided as follows:

Class *Chondrichthyes* (Cartilaginous Fishes)

Order (1) Cladoselachii—ancestral sharks
Order (2) Pleuracanthodii—early freshwater sharks
Order (3) Selachii—marine sharks
Order (4) Batoidea—skates and rays
Order (5) Holocephali—shark-like fishes sub-divided into two
sub-orders as follows:
Sub-order (1) Bradyodonti—late Palaeozoic forms
with strong dental plates, and
Sub-order (2) Chimaerae—the rat-fishes

The chondrichthyoids first appeared in the Upper Devonian, flourished during the Carboniferous and continue to the present day, being represented by the modern sharks and dogfishes, skates and rays, and rat-fishes. Their endoskeleton is entirely cartilaginous —a feature which, as we shall see later, confers some distinct advantages as well as possessing certain drawbacks—and their exoskeleton consists of placoid denticles, which may sometimes be enlarged into head-spines or fin-spines. The fin-webs in most species are supported by horny fin-rays or *ceratotrichia*, but bone is never present.

An important feature of this group, absent in all other fishes, is the presence of a *spiracle* in front of the anterior gill-slit. There may be from five to seven gill-slits, and there is no operculum, except in Holocephali. The mouth is ventral; the teeth are typically not fused to the jaws, and replace one another serially. Most important of all, the hyomandibular, which derives from what was ancestrally the first branchial arch, plays an important part in the suspension of the jaw apparatus.

The Chondrichthyes are an essentially predaceous group, relying on their sense of smell rather than sight for the locating of their prey. Consequently the eyes are small in proportion to the head, while the olfactory capsules are relatively large and well-developed, the nostrils being more or less ventrally-situated.

The lateral line runs between two rows of denticles, passing forward to the head, where it joins the infra-orbital canal. The supra-orbital canal is connected dorsally with this canal both behind and in front of the eye.

Despite the fact that the cartilaginous nature of the endo-skeleton renders any fossil remains in this group except teeth, scales or spines exceedingly rare, the evolution of the chondrichthyoids, in broad outline, is fairly well understood. Nevertheless, many of the Palaeozoic families are still known only from their teeth and other isolated parts.

The exact origin of this group, however, is far more obscure. While it seems not improbable that its ancestry may have placoderm affinities, difficulty immediately arises when it is considered how highly-specialised the latter were. It is possible, of course, that the chondrichthyoids may be neotenic descendants of one of the placoderm families which has retained the larval cartilage and fin-folds—a theory which is not so far-fetched as it sounds when these structures are compared.

The Cladoselachii or ancestral sharks

This, the most primitive group of all selachians, is most interesting for the type genus, *Cladoselache*, whose structure approaches a

condition to be expected in a hypothetical ancestral chondrichthyoid. The order is characterised by the presence of paired fins,
which are little more than triangular outgrowths of the body wall,
and by the absence of claspers in the males.

Cladoselache (Fig. 36) is the only really well-known member of
this group. It is a fairly large fish—a fully grown-specimen reaches
about 3 feet in length. The attenuated fusiform body is covered
by placoid denticles, which are enlarged around the eye to form an
orbital ring. The tail is markedly heterocercal, and there are two
dorsal fins, usually devoid of fin-spines. The paired fins, both pectoral
and pelvic, are lateral triangular flap-like structures similar to the
embryonic fin-folds of modern selachians.

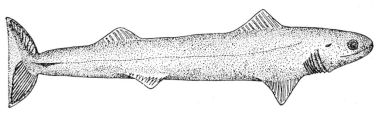

FIG. 36   *Cladoselache* (reduced)

The cartilaginous fin-supports are particularly characteristic.
All the fins have an endoskeleton of unjointed cartilaginous radials
and a row of basal cartilages. The vertebral column is devoid of
centra, the notochord being persistent.

The jaw suspension in *Cladoselache* is *amphistylic,* in which the
palatoquadrate has an otic and a basal process for articulation with
the neurocranium, which is platybasic and very similar in structure
to that of the living *Chlamydoselachus* : it differs markedly from that of
the placoderms in the shortness of the occipital region and the large
size of the olfactory capsules.

The teeth of these early ancestors of sharks are typical, having
one large central cusp and varying numbers of smaller lateral ones
(Fig. 37). Teeth of this type are very common in the early selachians
of Devonian and Carboniferous times, and it is on this evidence and
on the variety of structure shown in the few other known forms that
the group is presumed to have been a very large one.

D

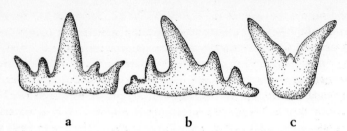

a   b   c

FIG. 37 Forms of teeth in fossil sharks: (a) *Cladodus*, (b) *Hybodus*,
(c) *Diplodus*

The Pleuracanthodii or early freshwater sharks

This is a fairly well-known group of moderate-sized fishes, easily
distinguished from the preceding group by the diphycercal tail
and the possession of claspers in the males, the elongated dorsal fins,
the divided anal fin and the presence of a cephalic spine at the
posterior end of the head. The dorsal fins are supported proximally
by at least two rows of radials, and distally by ceratotrichia. The
limb girdles are still primitive in having their right and left halves
unfused, as in the Cladoselachii. As in all primitive selachians, the
notochord is persistent.

The neurocranium in pleuracanthodians is essentially similar
to that of other selachians. The occipital region, however, is rather
more prominently developed in this group in relation to the
articulation of the cephalic spine. Jaw suspension is amphistylic,
and the dentition is peculiar to the group: there are two prominent
lateral cusps, both of which are larger than the single median cusp.

The Selachii or marine sharks

In this order the jaw suspension may be either amphistylic or
hyostylic, the palatoquadrate never being fused to the neurocranium.
The teeth, too, are typical: under microscopic examination they will
be seen to have an outer enamel-like layer, beneath which is a layer
of orthodentine containing numerous fine canals surrounding a
core of osteodentine. The teeth of Selachii replace one another
moderately quickly.

The Batoidea or skates and rays

Once the sharks had colonised the oceans, a vast increase of potential food-supply was opened up to them in the form of molluscs, and one group, the *Batoidea,* became modified for a mollusc-eating existence. Skates and rays are specially adapted for mollusc-feeding by having their mouths furnished with powerful crushing teeth; since molluscs are bottom-dwellers, the body in skates and rays has also become flattened to enable them to pursue a bottom-living existence. The pectoral fins have become greatly enlarged to form tremendous flap-like appendages at the sides of the body, in some types meeting each other in front of the head. The tail is greatly reduced, and in some cases bears a poisonous sting. The torpedo-rays have peculiarly modified muscles whose energy takes the form of electrical discharges, capable of delivering a severe electric shock. It is interesting at this juncture to note that what are thought to have been electric fields have been discovered in at least one of the most ancient ostracoderm types, particularly as the skates and rays are a comparatively modern offshoot of the chondrichthyoid stock, not appearing until the early Mesozoic.

The Bradyodonti

These were late Palaeozoic fishes with powerful dental plates, forming a sub-division of the Order *Holocephali.* These dental plates, with well-developed crushing powers and slow replacement succession, suggest a molluscan diet. They are characteristically devoid of an outer enamel-like layer, and their microscopic structure consists of numerous vertical parallel tubes of dentine, so that when the teeth are worn they exhibit a typical pitted appearance.

None of these fishes appear to have reached any great size. They were extremely abundant during the Palaeozoic, but most of the genera are known only from their teeth. In the few species which are known in greater detail, the males are furnished with claspers. The palatoquadrate is fused immovably with the neuro-cranium—a mode of jaw suspension known as *autostylic.* The two halves of the pectoral and pelvic girdles were not fused together, and the tail is heterocercal.

The Chimaerae or rat-fishes

This was another much later offshoot of the shark class, whose members are comparatively rare abyssal forms in modern seas. They have a small mouth furnished with stout crushing dental plates, and squids appear to form the greater proportion of their diet. These fishes were unknown until the commencement of the Trias, and are thought by many authorities to represent the degenerate descendants of one of the more advanced antecedent groups which had been both more extensive and more numerous, but there appears to be a considerable difference of opinion as to which group is the one most likely to have given rise to these relict forms.

IO

The Teeming Seas

THE Devonian era, aptly known as the Age of Fishes, marks the ascendency of the *Osteichthyes* or bony fishes, which constitute the vast majority of the members of their phylum. The most advanced group of bony fishes, the *Teleostei*, outnumber all other fishes twenty to one and all other land and water vertebrates combined—a measure of success attained by no other vertebrate group.

Soon after their first appearance in Devonian times the bony fishes rose to a position of dominance in fresh waters. The first forms were still heavily armoured, but in later types this feature gradually became reduced. Their most remarkable characteristic is the fact that the bones of the skull correspond almost precisely with the pattern of the arrangement of the bones of the human skull, with a few modifications.

Little is known with any degree of certainty of the actual ancestry of the *Osteichthyes* or bony fishes, though it would seem probable that they arose as an offshoot from the primitive sharks. The bony fishes are grouped as follows:

Class *Osteichthyes* (Bony Fishes)

Sub-class *Actinopterygii* (ray-finned fishes without internal nares)

Superorder (1) Chondrostei (retaining primitive characteristics throughout development)

Order (i)   Palaeoniscoidea (truly primitive forms, Palaeozoic)

Order (ii) Subholostei (progressive Triassic forms)

Order (iii) Polypterini (living African fishes, with much of the original Palaeoniscoid structure remaining)

Order (iv) Acipenseroidea (degenerate modern types)

Superorder (2) Holostei (mainly Middle Mesozoic, nearing extinction)

Superorder (3) Teleostei (from Late Mesozoic, now the dominant forms)

Sub-class *Choanichthyes* (fishes with internal nares)
  Order (i)   Crossopterygii (lobe-finned fishes)
                Sub-order (1) Rhipidistia
                Sub-order (2) Coelacanthini
  Order (ii)   Dipnoi (lungfishes)

Actinopterygii (ray-finned fishes without internal nares)

The *Actinopterygii* first appeared in the Middle Devonian, although it is thought that they may have had an earlier origin, this view being based on the occurrence of certain isolated scales found in Lower Devonian deposits, which may possibly have belonged to early fishes of this group. However, the precise origin of the actinopterygians is somewhat obscure; it is now generally accepted that both this order and the *Crossopterygii* (q.v.) are derived from a common origin.

The *Actinopterygii* form a very extensive and diverse group, which is represented at the present day by large numbers of living fishes. Since their origin they have evolved in such diverse and numerous ways that many of their more recent representatives have lost the essentially primitive features of the early members of the group.

The main points in which the *Actinopterygii* differ from the *Crossopterygii* are firstly, the absence of internal nares (nostrils); secondly, the arrangement of the dermal bones of the head and the course of the lateral line sensory system in the cephalic region; thirdly, the microscopic structure of the scales; and fourthly, the nature of the internal skeleton of the paired and unpaired fins.

In the lateral line system of actinopterygians a distinct jugal canal is absent, being represented only by a series of superficial pits, and the skull is completely devoid of any of the squamosal ossifications found in crossopterygians.

The scales are never cosmoid, but of the ganoid type, in which the entire scale lies beneath the skin. A typical ganoid scale consists of three layers: an outer dentine layer, a median layer of vascular bone, and an inner layer of lamellated bone or *isopedin*. As growth occurs on both outer and inner surfaces, the enamel-like dentine layer becomes replaced by a thick, transparent layer known as *ganoine*, the entire scale increasing in size concentrically. The scales are rhomboid and imbricating, articulating with one another by means of a dorsal extension on the upper edge of one scale fitting into a socket on the lower edge of the scale immediately above it.

There are no fleshy lobes to the paired fins, which are so typical of crossopterygians, nor is their internal skeleton concentrated into fused basal plates, but consists invariably of separate radials.

In broad outline the course of actinopterygian evolution is reasonably well-known, and has been reconstructed with a remarkable degree of accuracy. It has been possible to trace back all the later forms to a primitive basic type originating from the palaeoniscoid stock, and in the forward direction their evolution has culminated in the Teleostei, the dominant group of bony fishes to-day. During the Palaeozoic era the evolution of the *Actinopterygii* consisted, in the main, of modifications of ancestral palaeoniscoid characteristics, which Moy-Thomas has referred to as 'abortive attempts to achieve the holostean grade of structure'. Even as early as in Carboniferous times the primitive palaeoniscoid type showed a tendency to evolve in this direction, and by Permian times the first holostean, a form very similar to the living bowfin *(Amia)* of North America, had evolved. It is from fishes such as these that the Teleosts have arisen.

The Palaeoniscoidea or ancestral ray-finned fishes

The earliest bony fishes were the Palaeoniscoidea, which appeared in the Lower Devonian, attained their maximum development during the Carboniferous and Permian, and became extinct towards the end of the Jurassic. The palaeoniscoids exhibit such a combination of primitive features that they are now generally looked upon as the ancestors of all the later bony fishes, with the exception of the Crossopterygii. They are mostly elongated fusiform animals, with a large, markedly heterocercal tail, a single dorsal and a single anal fin. The body is completely enclosed in an armour of glossy ganoid scales, and the head is protected by a series of bony plates. The large mouth is armed with sharp-pointed teeth; most of these fishes were obviously fast-swimming predators. Although usually of small or moderate size, some palaeoniscoids reached a length of three feet or more.

The palatoquadrate is attached to the neurocranium by the hyomandibular. The conformation of the skull bears a general resemblance to that of the *Rhipidistia* (q.v.), but although an otic process is present it is never actually joined to the neurocranium. The hyomandibular articulates with the otic region of the neuro-cranium, sloping at a very oblique angle with the ventral end point-ing rearwards, allowing a very wide gape of the jaws.

The lateral-line runs forward to the head, where it joins its parallel structure from the other side in the occipital region.

Much diversity of form exists among these primitive palaeon-iscoids, and so far their family grouping is somewhat unsatisfactory. Most have rhomboid scales, triangular and acuminate fins, and deeply-cleft heterocercal tails. Typical members of the order include the Carboniferous *Rhadinichthys*, the Permian type genus *Palae-oniscus*, and the Lower Carboniferous *Phanerosteon*, which is singular in having lost most of its body scales, as in the modern sturgeon (*Acipenser*), a few scales remaining just behind the pectoral fin and in the caudal region. In contrast to this, the Lower Carboniferous *Cryphiolepis* has deeply-imbricating cycloid scales.

In the Upper Carboniferous genus *Phanerorhynchus* (Fig. 38) the skull, while generally of much the same structure as that of other palaeoniscoids, has a greatly-elongated snout-like rostrum, and the body scales tend to be large in size and relatively few, with promi-nent ridges on both dorsal and ventral surfaces. The most striking feature of *Phanerorhynchus*, however, is the great reduction in the number of fin-rays, which are spaced out and would seem to correspond in number to the internal radials. In this particular *Phanerorhynchus* approaches the *Holostei*.

Urosthenes is a peculiar Permian fish of which only the body is known. It is worthy of mention because here again there is an approach to the holostean condition, in the reduced number and wide spacing of the fin-rays. The tail is heterocercal; the body scales are cycloid and overlapping, but there are no dorsal ridge scales or fin-scales. These characters, together with the lobed nature of the unpaired fins, have led some authorities to believe that *Urosthenes* is actually a primitive crossopterygian, but the absence of an epi-chordal tail lobe and the presence of a single dorsal fin tend to refute this view.

The highly-specialised, deep-bodied *Dorypterus*, whose skeleton is shown at Fig. 39, approaches the holostean type of structure even more closely. The body is devoid of scales except in the caudal

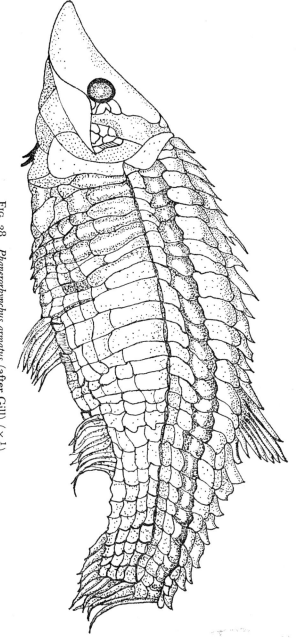

FIG. 38 *Phanerorhynchus armatus* (after Gill) ($\times \frac{1}{8}$)

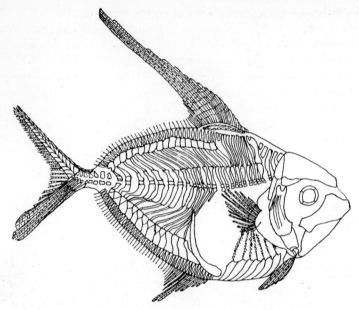

FIG. 39   Skeleton of *Dorypterus* (after Gill) ($\times \frac{1}{12}$)

region; from the illustration it will be seen that there is a great reduction in most of the dermal bones of the head, and there are no teeth. The internal skeleton of the paired and unpaired fins is, however, essentially palaeoniscoid in conformation.

The Chondrostei or primitive ray-finned fishes

As the Palaeoniscoidea were approaching extinction during the Lias, their place was taken by a small and comparatively unimportant order, the *Chondrostei*. This group had arisen from the main palaeoniscoid stem, and during the course of time, after a certain degree of modification, led eventually to the living sturgeons, which first appeared in Tertiary times.

The scales in chondrosteans, although ganoid in origin, have undergone considerable degeneration, but apart from this, and the presence of a series of branchiostegal rays and some other minor features, the modern sturgeons are not too unlike their prehistoric ancestors, typified by the type genus *Chondrosteus* and related forms.

The Subholostei or more advanced chondrosteans

Only a single true subholostean is known, the Upper Permian *Acentrophorus varians* (Fig. 40), which, although closely-related to the next group, the *Holostei,* possesses peculiar characteristics which set it apart sufficiently to justify its being classified in a separate order.

Acentrophorus is a small fish covered with cycloidal, imbricating ganoid scales. Although their microscopic structure has not been described, it is thought that they are modified from what is termed the 'lepidosteoid' type of scale found in some palaeoniscoids. In this kind of scale the cosmine and vascular layers have disappeared,

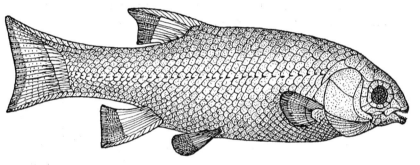

FIG. 40 *Acentrophorus varians* (after Gill) ($\times \frac{1}{12}$)

leaving only the outer ganoine, with its underlying layer of isopedin. (In the later bony fishes such as the Teleostei the ganoid layer also is lost, only the lamellated bone-layer remaining.)

All the fin-rays are reduced in number, and correspond with the internal radials. The tail is heterocercal, the axial lobe being reduced to a single row of scales.

The skull of *Acentrophorus* has many characteristic modifications. The jaw suspension is vertical, instead of oblique as in other related forms, and the maxilla is free at its hind end. Teeth are found only in the front part of the jaws.

The Holostei or intermediate ray-finned fishes

This is another small group, in which the fin-rays are reduced in number and correspond with the internal radials. The tail is heterocercal, the axial lobe being much reduced; in the later forms in this group this reduction has occurred still further, so that the tail is homocercal, the caudal fin being supported only by lepidotrichia.

There is a reduction in the maxilla and a modification of the opercular apparatus, with an additional gular bone, the *inter-operculum*, which appears to be formed by the displacement of the most dorsal gular. The premaxilla bears teeth, and is unconnected with the sensory canal, as in some palaeoniscoids. In modern holosteans the lateral line system differs from that of palaeoniscoids in that the supra-orbital canal does not continue backwards to join the parietals, but joins the infra-orbital canal in the post-frontal.

The neurocranium of holosteans includes a number of paired cartilages as well as bony structures.

The Teleostei or advanced bony fishes

The Teleostei embrace the vast majority of all living bony fishes (estimated at 97%), and although derived from the early ganoids they have during the course of evolution lost most of the primitive characters of their ancient forbears.

The body in teleosts is typically covered with thin cycloid or ctenoid scales, though sometimes bony scutes or, very occasionally, ganoid scales may be present. The entire endoskeleton is ossified, and the gills are freely suspended in a gill-cavity protected by a gill-cover or *operculum*. The tail is homocercal, and the pelvic fins may be either anterior to the pectorals or situated at any point elsewhere along the abdomen. The fin-rays may or may not be articulated. There are two pairs of nasal openings on the dorsal surface of the head.

Teleosts share with the ganoid fishes a hyostylic mode of jaw suspension. An important point of difference, however, is in the position of the preopercular, which never extends on to the face as in some ganoid fishes.

The *Teleostei* are sub-divided into several orders, but space does not permit of more than a brief mention of a few examples only. These various orders differ in such details as the presence or other-wise of a swim-bladder, the position of the pelvic fins, and the general shape of the body, which can be very divergent indeed from the commonly-accepted 'fish-shape' (e.g. eels, flatfishes, globe- and sun-fishes, John Dory, pipe-fishes and sea-horses).

It is noteworthy to point out at this juncture that the sea-horses do not appear to be represented in the fossil record.

The earliest teleost family is represented by the type genus *Semionotus* (Fig. 41), which flourished from the Trias to the early Jurassic. Unlike the active, predaceous palaeoniscoids which were their ancestors, the fishes of the genus *Semionotus* were slow swimmers, adapted for bottom-feeding on shellfish and the like, having a small mouth furnished with teeth of a more highly-specialised type. Just as adaptations in jaw conformation and dentition are related to a

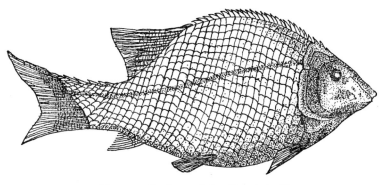

FIG. 41 *Semionotus* (after Fraas) ($\times \frac{1}{3}$)

different kind of diet, so variations in the form of the pectoral arch, median fins, and general body shape are related to different swimming habits (see Plate 12).

Another well-known and typical semionotid is *Lepidotus* (Fig. 42), whose dentition was highly-specialised. The palatine, vomer, maxilla and dentary carry rows of knob-shaped teeth, while the pre-maxilla is furnished with teeth of chisel-like form. *Lepidotus* ranged in time from the Middle Trias to the Cretaceous, and its teeth are very abundant fossils. Specimens of complete jaws have been found, exhibiting the curious manner in which the replacement teeth gradually turned over as they came into use.

During Triassic and Jurassic times the semionotids gave rise to a number of important offshoots, most of which flourished for a time and then became extinct by, or during, the Cretaceous era, with a few exceptions such as the gar pikes *(Lepidosteus)* and other highly-

FIG. 42   *Lepidotus* (reduced)

specialised forms. Among these extinct sub-groups were the
Pycnodonti, remarkable forms bearing a superficial resemblance to
the modern file-fishes *(Monacanthus* spp.*),* with deep bodies, small
mouths and specialised crushing teeth. Another interesting sub-
group were the *Eugnathi,* large-jawed predaceous types with fusiform bodies, many of which still had the ganoid scales of their
ancestors. The *Aspidorhynchoidea* were attenuated fishes with jaws
elongated into a beak-like extension, as in modern sword-fishes.
These are not, however, related to the gar pikes as formerly supposed,
the latter having, as we have already seen, derived much earlier in
time from the main stem and now considered to have descended
direct from the semionotid stock.

The Choanichthyes or lobe-finned fishes
This is the most important group of all fishes, as it includes the sub-
group from which the amphibians sprang, leading eventually to
the higher vertebrates and ultimately to man himself. Their
presence on Earth anticipated man's earliest immediate anthropoid
ancestors by some 400 million years, and all other vertebrates by
more than 100 million years. Many features of our human structure
were already present in these fishy ancestors of the incredibly remote
past, including the main plans and basic functions of all our organ-
systems.

We shall first look at the *Dipnoi* or lungfishes, before turning our attention to the *Crossopterygii,* one division of which bridges the seas of time between life in the water and the advent of first life on land.

The Dipnoi or lungfishes

The *Dipnoi* ('double-breathers') are an extremely long-lived group of fishes, which first appeared in the Middle Devonian and continue to the present day. During all this time a steady and easily-traceable evolutionary trend has taken place within the group, including a gradual loss of ossification and a degeneration of other characters, such as a return to continuous unpaired fins—a neotenic trait.

The Middle Devonian *Dipterus,* one of the best-known of these fishes, has several physical features which would seem to indicate that it is fairly closely-related to the *Rhipidistia* (q.v.). There are two lobed dorsals and an anal fin, and acutely-lobed, attenuated pectoral and pelvic fins. The tail is heterocercal, with a small epichordal lobe and a large hypochordal. The body scales are cycloidal and imbricating, and both the scales and the dermal bones are covered with a smooth cosmine layer. The conformation of the limb girdles does not differ from those structures in the *Rhipidistia*; the ribs are ossified, and the notochord is persistent.

The course of the sensory canals in the cephalic region is the same as that characteristic of rhipidistians, but the dermal bones are more numerous and may be in many ways considered to be more primitive. There is no maxilla or premaxilla; the absence of these bones is related to the peculiar dentition, which is entirely palatal. The palatoquadrate is much reduced and attached to the neurocranium (autostylic jaw suspension), and the hyomandibular is also reduced, being no longer functional in suspension. The parasphenoid is large, and covers almost the entire base of the neurocranium.

The neurocranium, while not differing radically from that of crossopterygians, is ossified into a single unit. This feature is particularly interesting, since the *Dipnoi* must have been to a great extent vegetable-feeders and so would not require the shock-absorbing apparatus found in their carnivorous relatives.

The Middle Devonian *Pentlandia* is very similar to *Dipterus* but shows some signs of approaching the condition of later forms. The posterior dorsal fin is larger and not lobed; the same applies to the Upper Devonian *Scaumenacia,* in which the epichordal lobe of the tail is larger, making the latter less heterocercal. In the Upper

Devonian *Phaneropleuron* the two dorsal fins and the epichordal lobe of the tail are confluent, the tail being diphycercal. Accompanying these changes there is also a reduction in both number and thickness of the dermal bones together with a loss of their cosmine layer, as well as of that covering the scales.

The *Dipnoi* are typically freshwater fishes, and their chief characteristic, from which the group takes its name, is that they can breathe either by means of their gills in the water, or by means of lungs on land. The lungs are formed by the connection of the swim-bladder with the gullet by means of a duct. In the living *Protopterus* of Africa there are external branchiae like those found in the larval stages of amphibians.

Ceratodus, a form allied to *Dipterus*, is one of the few instances of a fossil genus surviving until modern times, practically unchanged. Fossil teeth of *Ceratodus* had been known a long time, but it was not until 1870 that the existence of a living representative was discovered. The body is laterally-compressed, with one continuous vertical fin; the paired fins are paddle-shaped, with a broad fringe. The vomerine teeth are shaped like the incisors of many mammals, and the disposition of the palatal teeth differs only very slightly from that found in fossil types, in which these teeth were practically identical in form with those of the selachian *Notidanus*. The early *Ceratodus* reached a much greater size, however, than its living representative.

The cartilaginous nature of part of the skull has led many authorities to suppose that existing lungfishes are the most primitive of the dipnoans and more closely-related to the ancestral stock than the Palaeozoic forms such as *Dipterus*. In addition to the reduction in the number of dermal bones in the head, other degenerate features appear in the shape of the assumption of a more eel-like form and the extension of the median fins and their union to form a continuous fold round the hind end of the body. In the living *Protopterus* as well as the allied South American form *Lepidosiren*, the story has been carried a stage further: the paired fins are reduced to the point of being vestigial, and the scales are so embedded in the skin as to be invisible externally.

Respiratory characteristics of Choanichthyes

The incurrent and excurrent external nares of most fishes are generally situated in the *lateral* wall of the snout, their position corresponding with that of the external nostrils of tetrapods. In lungfishes, most sharks, and certain placoderms the two nasal openings are located in the *ventral* wall of the snout.

While in Devonian dipnoans the opening of the excurrent nostril was external, in living dipnoans this structure lies within the buccal cavity, as in the crossopterygians, thus giving rise to the name *Choanichthyes* (fishes with *choanae* or internal nares) for the group containing these two sub-divisions.

The air-breathing habit was established in Devonian dipnoans by the development of a lung, which opened as a blind sac off the ventral side of the oesophagus. This lung was functional in both primitive lungfishes and crossopterygians.

The Crossopterygii or lobe-finned fishes

The Rhipidistia

This is the group which, in Upper Devonian times, gave rise to the tetrapods—the first amphibians. Thus the fishes of this group are those from which all other terrestrial vertebrates, including ultimately man himself, evolved.

The Rhipidistia differ from other related groups in three main characteristics: in the number and arrangement of the dermal bones of the cephalic region, in having more lepidotrichia than radials in the caudal fin, and in possessing internal as well as external nares. They are additionally distinguished from the Dipnoi by having relatively few dermal bones in the roof of the cranium, and in the cheek region; they have a well-developed hyomandibular and simple conical teeth, the jaws being devoid of large grinding plates.

As far as the actual dermal bones of the head are concerned, the principal difference between the Rhipidistia and other related groups is the presence in the former of a maxilla, quadratojugal, and both lateral and median gulars. The Rhipidistia, which were generally large and voracious fishes, flourished from the Middle Devonian to the Lower Permian.

One of the most well-known rhipidistians is *Osteolepis* (Fig. 43), which is slender in body and has a markedly heterocercal tail, the hypochordal lobe being much larger than the epichordal; in some other types, however, the tail is diphycercal. The pectoral and pelvic fins may be obtusely lobed, or may have the lobes long and slender. The internal skeleton of the paired fins is so concentrated that a single basal element, the *humerus* (pectoral) or *femur* (pelvic) articulates with the limb girdle concerned, while the two more distal elements, the *radius* and *ulna* (pectoral) or the *tibia* and *fibula* (pelvic), articulate with the appropriate basal element. Here we have the basic plan of the tetrapod limbs, and thus in those incredibly remote waters the pattern was laid for the frog and the lizard, the bird and the rodent, the horse and the monkey, and ourselves.

The dorsal and anal fins of rhipidistians are also lobed, and have a concentrated internal skeleton, not unlike that of the paired fins,

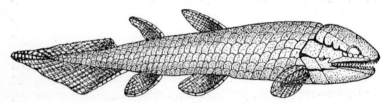

FIG. 43   *Osteolepis macrolepidotus* (after Pander) (reduced)

having a single proximal part with which the more numerous distal radials articulate.

The squamation in *Osteolepis* is rhomboid, the scales being fairly thick. Like the dermal bones of the head, the scales are covered with a smooth layer of cosmine which in the cephalic region frequently obscures the sutures between the bones. In certain forms, however, such as *Holoptychius* (Fig. 44), the cosmine is restricted to a few tubercles or ridges, the scales themselves being cycloid and imbricating. A section through a scale of *Megalichthys*, another interesting rhipidistian, is shown at Fig. 45.

In *Osteolepis* the axial skeleton consists of well-developed, ring-like centra, but in others such as *Eusthenopteron* the axial skeleton consists only of haemal and neural arches, the notochord being unconstricted. There are no ossified ribs.

One of the most characteristic features of the skull in rhipidistians is the division of the neurocranium into two parts—an anterior ethmo-sphenoid region and a posterior otic-occipital region. This

FIG. 44 *Holoptychius flemingi* (reduced)

sub-division also has the effect of separating the dermal bones of the roof of the skull into an anterior and a posterior shield. The reason for this sub-division appears to be to allow a certain degree of dorso-ventral flexure between the two parts of the skull. Although, from our knowledge of the skull conformation, this degree of flexure cannot have been very great, it probably served as a shock-absorbing mechanism when the fish snapped at its heavily-armoured prey. The teeth are fused to the bones of the jaws, and the palatal teeth frequently show exactly the same type of alternate replacement seen in the early labyrinthodont amphibians (q.v.).

The Coelacanths

The Coelacanths are a specialised group of crossopterygians, usually of small size but sometimes attaining four or five feet in length, as in

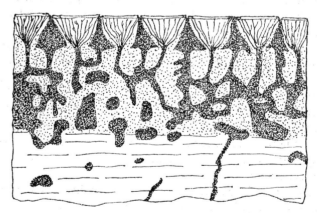

FIG. 45 Section through scale of *Megalichthys* (after Goodrich) ($\times 70$)

the case of the remarkable living *Latimeria*. The group has persisted from the Upper Devonian to the present day, practically unchanged; the living form differs only from its Upper Devonian forbears in the degree of ossification of the skull (see Plates 13–15).

Until 1938, all coelacanths were thought to have been extinct for at least 70 million years, until the fateful day when a living 5 ft. coelacanth was trawled off the eastern seaboard of South Africa.

On the 22nd December 1938 Miss M. C. Latimer, then curator of the East London Museum, was sorting through a pile of fishes just brought in to the quay by a trawling vessel when her attention was arrested by a curious bluish fish with limb-like fins and heavy ganoid scales, of a type she had never before encountered. Puzzled, she communicated with the late Professor J. L. B. Smith, the leading authority on fishes, of Rhodes University in Grahamstown, enclosing a sketch of the creature.

The impact of that rough sketch on Professor Smith was as though a bomb had burst in his brain. Those were his own words—and in fact at first his scientific reasoning could not, would not accept that this could be a real live coelacanth. What? Everyone knew the last coelacanths became extinct during the Cretaceous. Surely Miss Latimer must be mistaken! Doubts nagged at him day and night. He must go to East London, the holiday season and its inevitable traffic delays notwithstanding, to see the fish for himself.

Yes! It was an undoubted coelacanth—and thus the most fantastic event in the history of the science of living things exploded on the world. Biologists could not have been more amazed if they had seen *Brontosaurus* ambling down the street.

Professor Smith named the coelacanth *Latimeria chalumnae*, the new genus being founded in honour of Miss Latimer, whose foresight had saved this treasure for science instead of allowing it to be thrown away with a pile of assorted fishes already rotting in the tropical heat of a South African winter. The specific name refers to the fish having been caught off the mouth of the Chalumna River.

Let us now look at the modern Coelacanth—which is shown at Fig. 46—and compare it with the remote ancestors which it so closely resembles.

The coelacanths are heavily-built fishes, with paired external nares, limb-like paired fins ('Old Fourlegs'!) and two dorsal fins, only the posterior of which is lobed. The lepidotrichia of the anterior

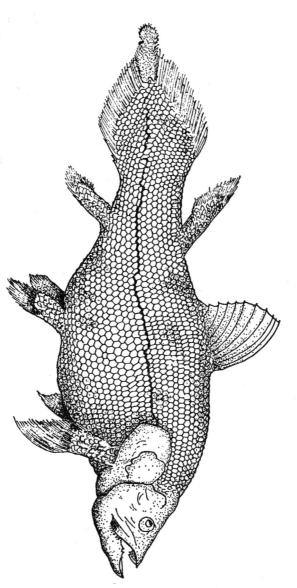

FIG. 46 *Latimeria chalumnae* Smith (× ⅛)

dorsal articulate directly with an internal plate-like skeletal element, while the lobed posterior dorsal has a concentrated internal skeleton, very similar to that of the paired fins.

The trilobate, diphycercal tail is one of the most characteristic features of the coelacanths. The lepidotrichia correspond in number with the radials; the notochord is persistent, and the haemal and neural arches have long slender spines, which are hollow (the word 'coelacanth' means 'hollow spine'). In some forms there are ossified ribs. The swim-bladder is calcified—a most curious feature which is characteristic of all the fossil forms—while in the living *Latimeria* the swim-bladder is vestigial. The scales are heavy and thick in the living coelacanth but thinner in fossil forms, in which the cosmine of both the scales and the dermal bones of the head is restricted to tubercles or ridges (cf. the rhipidistian *Holoptychius*).

In the primitive Upper Devonian coelacanths the neurocranium is ossified in two halves as in rhipidistians, but in later forms such as the Carboniferous *Rhabdoderma* and the Permian *Coelacanthus* the ossified parts consist of a paired ethmoid, a median sphenoid, and paired otic and occipital bones. In all forms, however, the skull is 'hinged', as it were, allowing a certain degree of dorsoventral flexure, as in the Rhipidistia. The hyomandibular is reduced, and it would appear that the palatoquadrate articulated only with the anterior part of the neurocranium.

The eyes are relatively large, and the arrangement of the ossifications of the orbit closely approaches that found in the labyrinthodonts. The dermal bones of the cheek region do not appear to articulate with one another very closely. There is no maxilla or quadratojugal, the dentition being confined to the pterygoid and palatine. The number of bones in the lower jaw is reduced, and there is only a single pair of large median gulars, but no laterals. There is no pineal foramen.

As I have already mentioned earlier, there is remarkably little evidence of change apparent in the coelacanths' evolutionary history, except for the gradual reduction of ossification in the neurocranium and the change in the method of articulation of the palatoquadrate. The survival of the coelacanth from the dim recesses of the past to the present day, all the while unsuspected by scientists until fortuitously rediscovered only 30 years ago, must indeed make us rather more cautious in future before we jump to conclusions about the supposed 'extinction' of this group or that. Only a few more coelacanths have turned up since *Latimeria* was discovered, and it was 14 years before a second coelacanth was caught despite arduous searching. Who knows, indeed, what other creatures known only from the remote past may still lurk in the depths of the ocean?

I always like to imagine one of those ancient crossopterygians struggling from the receding waters on to the Devonian mud, looking as astonished at seeing Man standing there as Man himself would if to-day he were to see one of these same extinct archaic creatures on the bank of a favourite fishing-spot, all the more so if he knew how many were the physiological similarities between them.

11

First Steps on Land

The rise of the amphibians

THE phrase 'missing link' has been bandied about for longer than most of us can remember. It started with Charles Darwin, whose theories shook the scientific world over 100 years ago. We have progressed a long way since then, but there are still tremendous gaps in our knowledge, most of which can be narrowed only by further discoveries in the record of the rocks. One thing, however, seems certain, and that is, that after millions of years in the waters the bony fishes were compelled to colonise the land, and that without this invasion there would have been no land-dwelling vertebrates. Exactly how and when this colonisation first occurred may never be known for certain.

The adaptation of water-dwelling forms to enable them to live on land did not take place overnight. The process, which had already begun in the Devonian era, was not completed until well into the Carboniferous. Some of the mechanisms essential for a terrestrial existence had indeed already developed—at least up to a point—in the primitive bony fishes. Lungs, for instance, are as important to land-dwelling animals as legs—perhaps more so; these were already present in the ancestral bony fishes.

The bony fishes, unlike the chondrichthyoids, had a well-developed bony skeleton, without which life on land would have proved impossible. A vertebral column and limb supports of cartilage are perfectly capable of supporting an animal in the water, but they are utterly inadequate to support a heavy body on land.

Potential land adaptations having already been initiated, one is tempted to think that nature had the evolution of the amphibians in mind before the emergence of the group; but that is rather like putting the cart before the horse. There are two schools of thought about the colonisation of the land. Some scientists are convinced that the conquest of the land was intentional: 'Look at all that room on earth just waiting to be used!' So runs their line of reasoning; the waters were getting rather overcrowded anyway! It all sounds very logical—a neatly-devised hypothesis, until you come to think about it a bit longer.

Now let us look at the other side of the coin, represented by the views of the opposite camp. The fishes had always lived in the water; they had never been used to anything else. Why should they suddenly have an urge to live in an element of which they had neither knowledge nor experience? Assuming that they *could* support life on land, what would they do for food? There were no animals on earth at that time, and most groups were carnivorous. The few that were plant-eaters were accustomed to water-weeds and their kin—very different fare from a giant horsetail or cycad.

However, the lakes, streams, and estuaries of the late Devonian and early Carboniferous were greatly affected from time to time by periods of drought of long duration. During the great climatic upheavals of the time the sun would burn down relentlessly, drying up the waters, and fishes devoid of terrestrial adaptations would flounder helplessly in the mud and perish. It would therefore seem to be more reasonable to take the view that the development of lungs and limb-like paired fins was a built-in survival provision for just such eventualities. Legs were not for land-living, but for land-traversing to look for more water, lungs to breathe air to get them there! Our Devonian and Carboniferous ancestors first left the streams, the lakes and swamp pools to walk on land not from choice but from necessity.

The early amphibians were still not very far, evolutionally-speaking, from their crossopterygian progenitors. Internally many of their organs were identical; most of the early forms had long, tapering bodies and well-developed tails, and the majority had heavy bony armour on the head. The main difference was the adaptation of the paired fins into limbs and the ability to breathe air.

Another significant change was the modification of the hyomandibular, which is an integral part of the gnathic structure in fishes but in the amphibians has become specialised for a new function. Greatly reduced, it forms the small bone called the *stapes* situated in the internal ear. The problem of hearing on land is entirely different from the same problem under water; fishes have no special mechanism for transmitting external sounds to the internal ear, which is situated at some distance below the cranial surface. They are much more dependent on the lateral line sensory receptor apparatus which enables them to pick up vibrations in the water rather than sounds. On land, of course, an entirely different set of circumstances obtains.

The striking similarity of the arrangement of the bones in the amphibian limbs, already present, as we have seen, in the paired fins of crossopterygians, to the arrangement of the bones in the human limbs is at once apparent. This arrangement, both in the lobe-finned fishes and in amphibians, corresponds exactly to the pattern found in man, of one large proximal bone articulating at its distal end with two smaller ones, terminating in a further joint, beyond which are the five phalanges or fingers. Some amphibians, it is true, appear to have only four digits, but a closer inspection of the skeleton will reveal a fifth digit in vestigial form.

Paradoxically, therefore, the development of limbs and lung-breathing would seem to have been adaptations to enable the creatures concerned to remain in the water; but it is not hard to visualise how true terrestrial existence came about. The amphibian, looking for a fresh pool or stream, might wander miles off course, and meanwhile have to maintain life somehow until water was reached. Perhaps water never was found; it might have been too far away, so that the animal would have been compelled to nibble vegetation to keep going. The first entirely land-living animals, the reptiles, were mainly herbivorous, and it is not difficult to see why. By the time the reptiles had evolved from the amphibian stock in Mesozoic times there were, it is true, quite a few other forms of animal life on earth, although reptiles were then dominant; so a few groups became carnivorous and, as always, larger forms would eat smaller forms, including members of their own group. Thus true land-living groups gradually became established as a consequence of these various developments, each with its own particular niche in the food chain.

Let us now look at some of the sub-divisions of the Amphibia and their characteristics.

The living Amphibia comprise three very highly-specialised orders: the frogs and toads, the newts and salamanders, and the caecilians, which are a small and inconspicuous group or rare, burrowing worm·like forms found in the tropics. A further group, the labyrinthodonts, which were the earliest amphibians, became extinct during the Trias.

Amphibians ('two ways of life') are able to breathe by means of gills in the water and lungs on land. In some forms gills are present only in the juvenile stages and disappear in the adult. The moist skin of adult terrestrial forms plays an important part in the respiration cycle, enabling the animal to absorb oxygen from its surroundings. The amphibians, though able to leave the water during at least some part of their adult lives, are ultimately still dependent on it for survival: without a moist habitat they will die of desiccation, and they must return to the water to breed.

In existing forms the cranium is always articulated to the vertebral column by means of two distinct exoccipital condyles, but in a few of the early labyrinthodonts these were not ossified. The jaw suspension is autostylic, as in the Dipnoi (q.v.); a large parasphenoid is invariably present.

The vertebral column is more or less completely ossified, and can generally be differentiated into cervical, dorso-lumbar, sacral and caudal regions; the sacrum, however, usually consists of only one vertebra. The sternum, which is never present in fishes, occupies a central position in the thorax; the pectoral and pelvic girdles are well-developed. The pubis is frequently cartilaginous, and when it is ossified it is always smaller than the ischium, which more often than not is united with the pubis, whether or not the latter is ossified.

Limbs may be entirely absent, as in caecilians, or well-developed, varying greatly in their proportionate length, as in frogs.

Teeth are normally present on the premaxilla, maxilla, vomer and dentary, but are usually wanting on the palatine and pterygoid in living forms, though present on both pterygoid and parasphenoid in labyrinthodonts. These teeth are usually anchylosed to the bone, and in existing forms are simple in structure, while in labyrinthodonts they are usually very much more complex owing to foldings of the dentine, this being an extreme development of that met with in certain ganoid fishes.

Normally there is no exoskeleton in living forms, though in most labyrinthodonts bony scutes were generally present, usually restricted to the ventral surface of the body.

Affinities between the Amphibia and the early ganoid fishes

are apparent. Evidence of relationship with the primitive ganoids is clearly shown in the labyrinthic structure of the teeth and in the paired supra-occipital ossifications, neither of these two features being found anywhere else in the entire animal kingdom. The vertebral column, too, is similar in structure to that found in early ganoid fishes.

While the labyrinthodonts flourished from the Carboniferous to the Trias, the *Anura* (frogs and toads) did not evolve until the Cretaceous, and the other two orders are even more recent in origin, the newts and salamanders not occurring until the Tertiary, and caecilians being unknown until the present epoch. It is thought that the reptiles, which were the next step along the evolutionary road, evolved from the labyrinthodonts, evidence being based on such features as the complete separation of the pterygoids in the median line (cf. *Pariasaurus*), the absence of an obturator foramen *(ibid)*, and certain complex features of the external bones of the skull and of the pectoral region which are exactly similar to the corresponding structures in crocodilians. A typical labyrinthodont, the Permian *Euryops*, whose skeleton is shown at Fig. 47, will be seen to bear a superficial resemblance to a generalised crocodilian; indeed, many of its body structures will be found to be basically similar.

From the ganoid fishes to the labyrinthodonts, the first amphibians, was but one step part of the way across the vast bridge leading from complete dependence on the water to adaptation for a fully terrestrial existence, which was essential if a class of animals were to be successful as a group. No group could hold its own in the face of changing

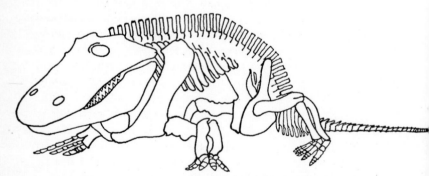

FIG. 47   *Euryops,* a typical labyrinthodont (after Colbert)

conditions unless it could become independent of a restricted, and restricting, habitat. The amphibians formed the spearhead to point the way; but it was their descendants, the reptiles, that finally broke free from the tyranny of the waters, and established independent life on earth.

12

The Colonisation of the Land

The first reptiles

WHEN the first pioneers went out to colonise the Wild West or the Australian outback, what was the first thing they did, or attempted to do? Why, to reproduce as nearly as possible in their new environment the familiar conditions of comfort to which they had been accustomed at home. They had never been nomads sleeping out under the stars, or even under canvas: they had been accustomed to living in houses, in permanent settlements. So they built townships of houses for themselves and their families, providing protection in winter from the bitter cold, the high winds and the driving rain, and shelter in high summer from the burning sun.

It needs little stretching of the imagination to visualise that the amphibian, whose life was so inexorably bound up with the water, would need to take the water with it, as it were, to enable it to feel at home on dry land. The two main points, we recall, of this amphibian subservience to the water were that its body must not be allowed to become desiccated, and that it was compelled to return to the water to breed.

The amphibian egg consisted of the embryo, together with its yolk or food-store, surrounded by a jelly-like protective covering which swelled up and kept the egg buoyant in the water which surrounded it. Now, if the amphibian could produce an egg in which the embryo and its yolk could be surrounded by water as well as by a protective covering, then one problem at least could be very neatly solved, and a group of animals which could produce such an egg would be half-way to being able to live entirely out of the water.

Let us look at the stylised diagram of the amniote egg at Fig. 48. The embryo will be seen to be surrounded by a membranous sac, the *amnion,* containing a liquid, the *amniotic fluid,* which completely surrounds the embryo, except at the point where it is joined to the yolk or food-supply. In other words, the embryo with its food-store is surrounded by water, just like frog or newt spawn, the jelly-like covering having been modified to form the amniotic membrane.

While the frog or newt embryo was able to obtain oxygen from the water and to excrete carbon dioxide and other wastes by osmosis, provision now had to be made for these processes in the amniote egg. So the *allantois* was formed, acting both as a means of obtaining oxygen and as a mechanism for the excretion of wastes.

There was still the question of protection from desiccation and injury to an egg laid on land to be taken care of; so the *chorion* and the *shell* were evolved to solve this problem. (In mammals, whose young are born alive, the chorion has become modified to form the *placenta* whereby the embryo derives nourishment from the mother while in the womb or uterus.)

The need for an aquatic stage now having been eliminated, the embryo of an emancipated amphibian could now develop towards terrestrial life when sufficiently advanced in growth to hatch and support an independent existence. But now another problem arose: how to live on dry land without desiccation. Somehow, loss of moisture by evaporation through the skin must be prevented. The new colonists of the land, therefore, had to have some kind of protective covering for the skin; so gradually it became cornified, fre-

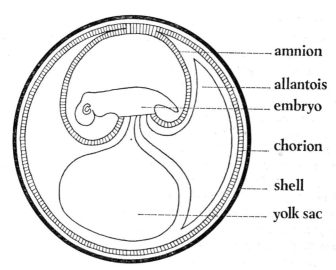

amnion

allantois
embryo

chorion

shell
yolk sac

Fig. 48   Diagram of an amniote egg (after Roemer)

quently covered with overlapping scales, and thus body moisture was prevented from escaping, the body's fluid balance being maintained by metabolic processes such as respiration and excretion.

Let us now look at some of these early pioneers, the first traces of which appear in the Carboniferous, when the amphibians were at the zenith of their development.

The problematical *Seymouria*, a somewhat unprepossessing creature about two feet in length, is of Lower Permian origin, but is still very little further advanced than the lesser-known ancestral forms from the Carboniferous which preceded it. The structure of its skull, its dentition, and certain vertebral characteristics are still typically amphibian, while its mode of jaw suspension, the conformation of the pectoral girdle and limbs, and certain other features of the axial skeleton are essentially reptilian. What, therefore, is *Seymouria*? Is it an amphibian, or is it a reptile? No one is quite certain, because no one has as yet found out whether it laid its eggs in the water or on land. If it laid an amniote egg on land, it was a reptile; if not, it was an amphibian. It is as simple as that.

Seymouria is not considered to be the direct ancestor of the reptiles, which is hardly surprising, since we do not know for certain whether it can in fact be definitely classed as an amphibian or not.

The cotylosaurs or 'stem reptiles'

To be on the safe side one may look for true reptilian characteristics in a group which is known to have laid amniote eggs on land.

The *cotylosaurs* are the most primitive of known reptiles, first appearing in the Upper Carboniferous, and becoming extinct during Triassic times. They ranged in size from about a foot to ten feet in length, and their skulls and teeth were highly-specialised. An example is *Pareiosaurus*, from the Permian, which enjoyed a very wide global distribution. The heavy bodies of the cotylosaurs were supported by pillar-like legs, and these creatures were, strangely enough, vegetarians.

One of the characteristic features of the evolutionary development of a new major group of animals is the rapidity with which divergence occurs, producing a variety of different forms within the same group adapted to widely-differing types of habitat. This phenomenon, which is known as 'adaptive radiation', is particularly easily observed in the reptiles; although the cotylosaurs were the 'stem reptiles', many other groups evolved from them so rapidly, evolutionally-speaking, that they were still contemporaneous with the original 'stem reptile' stock before the latter became extinct.

One of these divergent groups, the *pelycosaurs,* is of particular interest as being the group from which the mammals later evolved. They were a very varied group, mostly of large size, some being more than ten feet in length. Their most striking characteristic feature was the huge sail-like fin that stood erect on their backs, supported by a series of greatly-elongated neural spines. Apparently this fin was, during life, covered with skin, and its probable function is still the subject of controversy. It could not have been of any sexual significance, for example, for display purposes to attract the opposite sex, as it was present in both sexes. One school of thought contends that this fin served to assist in the control of body temperature, while another more fanciful theory concludes that the supporting spines were in fact jointed or hinged so that the fin could be flapped from side to side, rather like a horse uses its tail, to swat irritating flies! *Edaphosaurus* stood over ten feet in length and was adorned with a 'sail' three feet high: woe betide the luckless fly that got in its way!

Strange as it may seem, it was from these unwieldy pelycosaurs that the mammal-like reptiles evolved in Permian and Triassic times. But the day of the mammals was yet to dawn, even though their progenitors were already well-established. Now, the Mesozoic was the heyday of the reptiles, and it was the Mesozoic that saw the rise of the mighty dinosaurs, the greatest beasts that ever walked the face of the Earth. To trace their origins we must turn to the *thecodonts* or 'socket-toothed' reptiles, a group of great significance which gave rise also to many other groups such as crocodilians and birds.

The thecodonts were a very widely-distributed and varied group which flourished during the Trias. Usually relatively small in size, they had hollow teeth set into deep sockets in the jaws (hence the name of the group), and many of them had their bodies protected by bony scutes. One interesting branch of this group, the *phytosaurs* or 'plant (-eating) lizards', were aquatic crocodile-like herbivores, some of which reached twenty feet in length from snout to tail. Although they lived in lakes and streams like modern crocodiles,

E

and even looked like crocodiles, they were not the ancestors of these animals. Their superficial resemblance is the direct result of similar adaptation to the environment common to both (though at different times)—an excellent example of what is known as *parallel evolution*, in which entirely unrelated groups of animals acquire similar characteristics in similar environments even though widely-separated by time, geographical distribution, or both.

The main group of thecodonts, however, were very different from these divergent phytosaurs. They were small, active, terrestrial forms, which frequently adopted a bipedal habit. This change of posture led to extensive and far-reaching physiological changes throughout the entire body. The hind limbs became longer and stronger, the pelvic girdle becoming adapted to support the entire weight of the body. The forelimbs were progressively reduced, while the long tail was used in maintaining balance.

From these small and inoffensive vegetation-eaters, some of which were little bigger than a domestic cat, the mighty *Brontosaurus* and *Diplodocus* and their kin evolved, for which Sir Richard Owen in 1842 coined the term 'dinosaurs', or 'terrible lizards'. And terrible indeed they must have been as they roamed the Earth in their heyday, unquestioned lords of creation.

13

The Dominance of the Reptiles

The Age of Dinosaurs

THE dinosaurs were the most spectacular creatures that ever lived. The greatest of them all, *Tyrannosaurus rex*, the 'King of the Ruling Lizards', measured no less than 50 feet long and stood 20 feet high at the shoulder. Now, I am an ardent herpetologist, but I would unquestionably not like to encounter *Tyrannosaurus rex* if he should happen to turn up again, like the 'extinct' coelacanth. This, however, is hardly likely, for whereas Old Man Coelacanth could, and did, lurk unsuspected for centuries, a creature of such gigantic proportions as *Tyrannosaurus rex* could scarcely go unnoticed for long. However, all dinosaurs were not as big as the 'King of the Ruling Lizards'; some true dinosaurs, in fact, were little bigger than a domestic chicken. So one never knows what may one day turn up—although all the evidence points to the dinosaurs having died out by the end of the Cretaceous. I must try not to sound too optimistic, but that is exactly what scientists said about the coelacanth, too. . . .

The dinosaurs fall naturally into two main sub-divisions, the carnivorous *saurischians,* of which *Tyrannosaurus rex* was monarch, and the *ornithischians,* which were plant-feeders.

The first saurischian dinosaurs appeared in the Upper Trias and were directly descended from the thecodonts. While some were comparatively small in size, others, as we have seen, reached gigantic proportions. Long before *Tyrannosaurus rex* thundered through the Cretaceous, the Jurassic *Allosaurus,* 35 feet long, was striking terror into its herbivorous contemporaries such as *Brontosaurus,* whose crushed remains have been discovered in close proximity to teeth of *Allosaurus.* The skull of *Tyrannosaurus rex* was four feet long, and some of its dagger-like teeth were six inches in length; those of *Allosaurus* could not have been much smaller if it could kill and devour a creature the size of the massive *Brontosaurus,* leaving only the broken bones.

These monsters had powerful claws on their hind limbs, on which they moved bipedally, the forelimbs being absurdly tiny, hand-like appendages. The tail, which was heavy and tapering, was used for balance, rather like that of a kangaroo.

Although the saurischians as a group were in the main carnivorous predators, they gave rise to an offshoot branch, the *sauropods*, which flourished during the Jurassic and Cretaceous. Surprisingly, the sauropods were not only inoffensive plant-eaters but at the same time reached even greater dimensions than the carnivorous saurischians. Some of them were more than eighty feet in length and weighed upwards of 50 tons, and were the largest land animals ever to have lived.

Typical examples of sauropods are *Brontosaurus* and *Diplodocus*, whose bodies were supported on massive, pillar-like legs, the shorter forelimbs being an obvious legacy of their thecodont lineage. The long tail, as in the saurischians, afforded additional support to the body; the neck, too, was very long, but the head was extremely small in proportion to the body. These animals probably spent their time partly submerged in lakes and rivers, rather like the hippopotamus, browsing on various kinds of vegetation. Evidence for this is found in the greater concentration of weight in the posterior part of the skeleton, which would promote stability in the water, and in the situation of the eyes and nostrils on the top of the head, enabling the animals to breathe and keep a lookout for their enemies while almost completely submerged. Their watery habitat also provided a quick means of escape should the enemy strike.

By the end of the Jurassic the so-called 'amphibious' sauropods (which were, of course, reptiles and not amphibians) had reached their peak, and as the Cretaceous dawned over the Earth their decline was already setting in. As they waned and finally died out, the other great dinosaur group which had evolved from the thecodonts took over. These, the *ornithischians*, unlike their saurischian cousins, were herbivorous *ab initio*. Mainly bipedal, their locomotion might well have included a stroll or two on all fours when in slow motion, since their forelimbs were but little reduced.

The 'duck-billed' dinosaurs

In many ornithischians the toothed anterior part of the jaws was replaced by a hard, horny, bird-like beak. The teeth in the

FIG. 49 *Stegosaurus*, an ornithischian dinosaur

posterior part of the jaws were no longer pointed for tearing and rending, but were chewing teeth. A curious feature is the increase in number of these teeth; in some forms, known as the 'duck-billed' dinosaurs, the 'bill' was furnished with anything from 1500 to 2000 teeth!

The 'duck-billed' dinosaurs were abundant during the Cretaceous. They had webbed feet and, like the sauropods, inhabited pools and swamps, feeding on aquatic or marginal vegetation. A typical example is *Iguanodon,* which was 25 feet long and stood 15 feet high, and was the first dinosaur, incidentally, to be described.

Armoured types
Since all the ornithischians were herbivorous, their only use for speed was to enable them to escape from their carnivorous enemies. As time went on, several groups of ornithischian dinosaurs reverted to a quadrupedal gait, though still retaining the shorter front limbs

of their thecodont ancestors. These ponderous, slow-moving types would have been too vulnerable to attack without some form of protection, so they developed armour against the depredations of the great carnivores. The *Stegosaurus*, for example, which is shown at Fig. 49, sported a double row of stout bony plates along the length of the back, and two pairs of sharp spike-like projections near the tip of the tail. A later form, the smaller *Ankylosaurus*, had the skull reinforced with bony plates and the body covered with a protective layer of ossified scutes, from which spines projected along the sides.

The horned dinosaurs

The horned dinosaurs appeared later in time than most of the other forms, being confined to the Upper Cretaceous. They had massive bony head-shields furnished with horns, but the body was left comparatively unprotected: everything had gone to their head, as it were. A broad protective bony plate extended over the nape of the neck (a frequent target for attack), and horns, presumably for defence, were developed on the frontal regions of the head, usually in the form of a pair situated above the eyes, much as in cattle, and a third horn on the nose like the rhinoceros.

Triceratops, 25 feet long, was the last of these great horned reptiles, and one of the last of the long line of the dinosaurs. The great head shield of *Triceratops* was over six feet long—almost one quarter the total length. It is of interest to note that in 1922 an expedition based on the American Museum of Natural History discovered in Mongolia several well-preserved clutches of eggs of the earliest of the horned dinosaurs, the ancestral *Protoceratops*, in some of which unhatched embryos had been perfectly preserved.

The decline of the ruling reptiles

By the end of the Cretaceous all the dinosaurs had disappeared from the face of the earth, and the great Age of Reptiles, which had ruled the land for 150 million years, was at a close. Destined not to survive, despite their supremacy during their heyday, they left no descendants, for the reptile groups which flourish to-day are direct heirs of the thecodonts, evolving as separate branches from the ancestral thecodont stock and not by way of the dinosaur lineage.

What factors were dominant in hastening the demise of the

great monsters which have so captured the human imagination ever since their discovery? No single cause can be put forward, but rather a combination of contributing factors. The carnivorous dinosaurs would have died out with the extinction of the herbivorous types upon which they preyed; these latter probably gave up the unequal struggle in the face of changing climatic conditions which led to the disappearance of their normal food and its replacement by other types of plants to which they did not have time to become adapted.

Many dinosaurs were inhabitants of lowland swamps and lakes, and doubtless as vast areas of the   territories rose during the land upheavals which took place at the end of the Cretaceous period the dinosaurs found themselves literally high and dry. In North America, at least, it is known that definite climatic changes took place at this time, caused directly by major geophysical events such as the rise of the Rockies and other mountain systems. Such cataclysmic upheavals could not fail to have far-reaching effects on the plant and animal life, through altered climatic and physical conditions.

When only the successful could survive

Although the ill-fated dinosaurs were the most conspicuous they were by no means the only descendants of the thecodonts. The crocodiles, too, had evolved and, in their inconspicuous way, were plodding ponderously in the Triassic mud long before their larger and more impressive brethren crashed across the scene in later times.

The earliest true crocodile was *Protosuchus,* a heavily-armoured, lizard-like creature about three feet long. During subsequent ages its descendants took over the environments formerly inhabited by the phytosaurs (described in Chapter 12) and achieved a widespread global distribution, becoming highly-specialised to enable them to pursue a predatory life in pools and streams. The largest of these early crocodiles were *Deinosuchus* and *Rhamphosuchus,* both of which attained a length of 30 feet. Can you imagine a crocodile almost the length of two London buses? I thought the Nile crocodiles I saw at close quarters when I was in West Africa were quite big enough!

The crocodiles have undergone little radical change since the

Mesozoic; they are still a successful, if somewhat limited, group. The lizards, too, are not unsuccessful as a group, though comparatively unprogressive from an evolutionary point of view. They are the most abundant of living reptiles, and have retained to a great degree the primitive type of locomotion characteristic of the salamanders. Their limbs, however, are much more lightly-built, and many lizards are capable of moving at incredibly fast speeds. The largest lizard now living is the Komodo dragon, one of the monitors, which can grow up to ten feet in length.

The lizards are an extremely varied order and include the grotesque chameleons, the limbless burrowing forms such as the slow-worm, the Galapagos marine iguana, and the Gila monster, the only venomous lizard in the world.

A side-development from the lizard stock culminated in the snakes, which have abandoned limbs altogether and reverted to the sinuous twisting of the body which characterises the locomotion of their remote fishy ancestors. It is as well to point out here that the slow-worms and other limbless lizards are quite unrelated to snakes, ancestrally-speaking, and in fact on dissection the limbs of 'legless' lizards will be found within the body in vestigial form. However, it is in the conformation of the skull that the snakes diverge most widely from the lizards. In snakes the skull is greatly modified, and the jaws are attached to the skull only very loosely, being capable of tremendous expansion. The potential gape is so wide that a snake only a few feet long can swallow a rabbit in its entirety, while a large boa constrictor or python is capable of engulfing an antelope whole.

Snakes are rare as fossils, owing to the extreme delicacy of the skeleton, but it is thought that they first evolved in the late Cretaceous as an offshoot of the monitor-type lizards. All the early snakes were heavily-built, constrictor-like forms, and fossil skulls with poison fangs have not been discovered in deposits of earlier age than those of Miocene origin.

The rhynchocephalians

The *rhynchocephalians*, a persistent but unimportant group dating from Triassic times, are represented to-day only by the tuatara *(Sphenodon)* of New Zealand, which is the only survivor of the much larger and more stockily-built Middle and Upper Triassic rhynchoce-phalians, which had toothless, beak-like jaws. Superficially the tuatara greatly resembles 'ordinary' lizards, but its archaic features, unchanged through millions of years from those of its Triassic ancestors, justify its being retained in the order *Rhynchocephalia* and separated from the true lizards.

The tuatara is frequently referred to as a 'living fossil', which is indeed an apt description. In the temporal region are *two* foramina, instead of only one as in all modern lizards. The only other reptiles known to have had these two openings in the skull—apart from the fossil rhynchocephalians—are the extinct dinosaurs. These two foramina are separated by a complete arch of bone, to which the quadrate is attached connecting it with the lower jaw. (In the true lizards the quadrate is free at its lower end, allowing some movement in the upper jaw.) Where the frontals and the parietals meet in the roof of the skull there is a small gap, and beneath this lies the pineal or 'third eye', which is part of a complex organ situated above the brain. Some of the primitive fishes such as the lampreys have a similar organ, but it is more elaborately developed in *Sphenodon*; it has a lens and a retina (a phototropic or light-sensitive layer), but no iris. The pineal eye is very minute, being no more than 0·53 mm in diameter. The surface of the lens is covered by a translucent membrane, which is continued to fill the remainder of the pineal foramen.

The 'third eye' seems to have no use as an optical organ, since not only has the nerve leading from this structure to the brain degenerated, but the pineal foramen is completely covered by skin and scales. The position of the pineal eye is, in fact, visible only in newly-hatched and very young specimens, in which its position is indicated by an irregularly-shaped, transparent scale surrounded by other larger scales arranged radially.

Another unique feature of the tuatara is the absence of any intromittent sexual organ in the male, unlike lizards and snakes, which have paired organs, the *hemipenes*. Neither are there any external ear openings in the head. Other peculiar features include the concave surfaces of the vertebrae, the hook-like processes of the ribs, the series of bony rod-like structures in the abdominal wall (the abdominal ribs), and the primitive teeth, which are not separate structures set into sockets but are merely serrated edges of the upper and lower jawbones; obviously these 'teeth' cannot be replaced, and so gradually become worn almost flat with advancing age. There are also present some additional palatal teeth, and a pair of greatly-enlarged teeth in the front of the upper jaw. None of these features is found in any lizard.

Another point too noteworthy to be overlooked is the fact that the metabolic rate of the tuatara is the lowest of all reptiles. No other reptiles exist either in tropical or temperate regions which have a lower body temperature than 58°F., while the body temperature of the tuatara is maintained at 52°F. The rate of the tuatara's breathing, too, is much less than that of any other vertebrate. An active tuatara was observed by one research worker for over an hour, during which time no breathing occurred.

The return to the waters

It is perhaps strange to realise that although the reptiles were the first animal class to become firmly entrenched on land, some of them eventually returned to the waters. This trend can also be observed in other animal groups; in fact it is one of the most constant features of evolution that once the members of any group have become established in a particular environment, some of them tend to spread into other completely different types of habitat, even to the extent of recolonising types of environment long since abandoned by the rest of their kind.

The body changes necessary for this re-adaptation are frequently just as radical as those which were needed to abandon the same type of habitat earlier in the group's history; but the end-product of this re-adaptation seldom bore much resemblance to the original colonists. Thus, the reptiles which later returned to the waters did not become fishes again or even amphibians, but modified reptiles. Once a structure has been replaced in any animal group, the genetics of natural selection ensure that nothing similar to the original structure will reappear: the process of evolution is irreversible. There may well be, of course, certain superficial resemblances between different life-forms sharing a common mode of existence, for example, sharks and dolphins; outward form needs to be similar merely to facilitate movement through the water. But there the resemblance ends. This is what zoologists refer to as 'convergent' evolution.

The ichthyosaurs

The extinct *ichthyosaurs,* which superficially were not unlike sharks or dolphins, are a case in point. Sharks are fishes and dolphins are mammals, but the ichthyosaurs, or 'fish-(like) reptiles', were true reptiles. First appearing in the Middle Trias, they were streamlined creatures about ten feet long, with elongated snout-like jaws armed with sharp teeth, large eyes, two pairs of paddle-like ventral limbs, and a fleshy dorsal fin. In the earliest forms the tail was long and pointed, but in later types it became fish-like with the vertebral column continued into a hypochordal lobe. This tail was used mainly as a propeller, the limbs being used for steering.

Some remarkably well-preserved fossils of ichthyosaurs have turned up which have provided irrefutable evidence that the ichthyosaurs were viviparous, i.e., they gave birth to living young. Fast and powerful swimmers of the open seas, they were one of the most successful of the aquatic reptilian groups, persisting until Upper Cretaceous times.

Several other aquatic reptile groups flourished during the Mesozoic before finally becoming extinct. One of these groups was the *plesiosaurs,* found throughout the Jurassic and Cretaceous, some of them reaching 50 ft. in length. Like the ichthyosaurs, the plesiosaurs had paddle-shaped limbs and sharp teeth; some were short-necked with huge heads (the skull alone of one form exceeds ten feet in length), while others had long necks (sometimes twice the length of the body) with smaller heads. All these creatures were rapacious carnivores, subsisting on fishes, until changing conditions at the close of the Cretaceous brought about their doom.

The Chelonia (tortoises and turtles)

The *chelonians,* which first appeared in the Trias, were at first all freshwater dwellers. Some of them later colonised the land, becoming the forerunners of our terrestrial tortoises, while a few, during Jurassic times, sought refuge from competition in the seas.

The first chelonians probably originated from *Eunotosaurus,* a small reptile of Permian times, whose ribs were greatly enlarged and modified to form a carapace, or dorsal shell. The earliest true turtles included forms with non-retractable heads and limbs, and at least one genus *(Triassochelys)* had teeth. These latter were lost in later types, which developed hard, horny, beak-like jaws and a heavy carapace formed by the development of dermal plates, some of which were fused to the ribs. This protective armour seems to be the basis of the survival of the turtles and tortoises through their long history; although in some ways a limited order, the chelonians are successful as a group.

Physiology of the chelonians

The armour of a turtle or tortoise is composed of two layers: a series of external horny scutes, representing the reptilian squamation, beneath which is a layer of bony plates. The joints between the component parts of each layer do not coincide; this alternation of joint sutures lends greater strength to the united structure. This principle has been adopted in bricklaying and other building processes to fortify the resulting structures.

The armour is divided into two sections, the upper shell or *carapace,* and the lower shell or *plastron.* The upper and lower sections of the shell are connected by 'bridges' at the sides, and the carapace is fused to the vertebrae along its central dorsal keel. On either side of this the lateral scutes are fused to the corresponding ribs, while further marginal rows complete the carapace and help to provide protection for the limbs.

The plastron is smaller and comprises fewer bony plates; in some living turtles the plastron is greatly reduced, as in *Macrochelys temmincki,* the American alligator snapper. The space between carapace and plastron is widest at the head end to enable the head and front legs to be extended or withdrawn during feeding and locomotion, while a narrower gap at the posterior end permits movement of the hind legs and tail. Some tortoises and turtles are able to withdraw head and legs completely within the shell, shutting themselves up like a box, by having either one, or in some cases two, hinges in the plastron, as in the mud and musk turtles of North America, or a hinged carapace, as in the land tortoises of the genus *Kinixys,* of Africa.

The gait of the terrestrial tortoises is awkward and lumbering, the limbs being splayed outwards. With the broad plastron protecting the belly, no other kind of locomotion is, indeed, physically possible. This kind of walking is typical of primitive land-dwellers such as salamanders, and apparently the early chelonians evolved their shells before improvements in locomotion had taken place.

Once the armour was finalised, so to speak, no improvement in walking method was possible.

The most primitive of living turtles are the *Pleurodira* or 'side-necked' freshwater turtles of the southern hemisphere. Their early ancestors did not have the power of drawing in their necks, and it was left to their later descendants to evolve this method of protection, drawing in the head by tucking the neck in sideways under the front edge of the carapace.

All other turtles and tortoises have evolved a different method of protecting the head. In these forms the head is withdrawn straight back under the front edge of the carapace without any visible bending of the neck, although actually the concealed part of the neck under the carapace bends sigmoidally in order to accommodate the head. For this reason these turtles and tortoises are grouped as the *Cryptodira* or 'concealed-necks'.

The land tortoises vary in size from small forms such as the familiar Greek tortoise of the pet-shops to the giants of the Galapagos and Aldabra, many of which weigh 500 lbs or more. Their longevity is proverbial; indeed, a creature so heavily-armoured and equipped for self-protection as the tortoise can have few natural enemies.

The trend towards an aquatic existence is strong in the chelonians. The mud and musk turtles and the snappers of North America are predatory bottom-prowlers in pools and streams; other types, such as *Pseudemys* and *Kachuga*, are river-dwellers. The softshells, or *Trionychoidae*, also river-dwellers, have lost their bony scutes and have a soft, leathery shell, their lack of protective armour being made up for by their fast swimming speeds and savage jaws. *Trionyx ferox* was not so named for nothing!

A few of the turtles returned to the sea, but even the largest of living marine forms, the leatherback *(Dermochelys coriacea)*, which at a record weight of 1960 lbs and a length of 10 ft 6 ins is the largest living reptile, is much smaller than the giant sea turtles which, together with the ichthyosaurs and the plesiosaurs, dominated the Jurassic and Cretaceous seas. One of these, *Archelon*, attained 12 feet in length; *Colossochelys* was even larger.

At first sight it might appear that *Dermochelys coriacea*, which is devoid of a hard carapace and has only a tough, leathery integument containing a series of small bony plates embedded in it, represents the most primitive chelonian type. However, the fossil evidence does not substantiate this, since the complete development of a hard bony carapace in chelonians was well-established by Triassic times, and the few imperfectly-preserved fossils which appear to represent early forms of *Dermochelys* do not occur earlier than in deposits of Eocene age. The most likely explanation is that the bony armour has become gradually reduced, as has happened in the evolution of other animal groups. *Dermochelys*, like all marine turtles, is a very fast and powerful swimmer, its huge body rendered buoyant by the depths of the tropical oceans which it inhabits, its paddle-like limbs shearing the water with hardly a sound as its streamlined form takes it along at speeds of anything up to thirty miles an hour. With such a means of defence *Dermochelys* would not really need the encumbrance of a heavy bony armour, which would only be an impediment in the water. In any case, a turtle of such a size would hardly have any natural enemies worth worrying about.

Finally, when discussing the aquatic chelonians, we must not forget that these animals, like all other reptiles, lay amniote eggs on land. At the breeding season the gregarious females congregate in great numbers on the shores and beaches, where they bury their eggs in the mud or sand, to be hatched several months later by the warmth of the sun. At this stage in the history of life parental care had not yet become a biological necessity; it was left to the birds, the first of the higher vertebrates to descend (or perhaps we should say ascend) directly from the reptilian stock, to develop this further refinement which was to lead to a greater economy of reproduction and conservation of the life-force itself.

14

Reptiles take Wing

Flying reptiles

THE development of the birds from the reptiles was a landmark in the evolutionary process, but this was not primarily, as one might think, a matter of merely throwing off the shackles of Earth and being able to fly and thus colonise greater expanses of territory. It went much further than that: it marked the beginnings of parental care of the young and laid the foundations for the family structure which was to be developed further in the mammals. This distinctive feature of avian reproduction can therefore be said to be the springboard from which the concept of group or community living took root, and the foundation of the relationships between individuals, families and societies which play so fundamental a role in the life of the higher vertebrates, including man.

In order to be successful as an animal group the birds had to evolve in such a direction that their body temperature could be regulated. An animal flying in the air would be seriously handicapped by having a poikilothermic blood-system, so provision had to be made for a constant temperature to be maintained whatever the temperature of the environment might be. The circulatory system, therefore, would have to be highly-specialised, and this was therefore the first of the evolutionary changes to be brought about, even more important to survival than the development of wings.

The senses of hearing and vision also needed to be more highly-developed, as an airborne animal would be much more dependent on these senses than the earthbound reptile, which was limited to crawling about in a relatively restricted environment.

The heavy scales of a reptile would prove a great handicap in flight, where lightness and mobility are of primary importance. If scales, now, could be modified to form feathers, another very important advantage would accrue: they would be able to trap air, which would not only assist in buoyancy, but also serve as an insulating layer and thus help to maintain body temperature.

The pterosaurs or 'winged lizards'

The *pterosaurs* were the earliest known flying vertebrates, appearing in the Jurassic and looking rather like large and clumsy lizards with bat-like wings.

The pterosaurs had three basic adaptations for aerial life: the modification of the forelimbs into wings, a light but strong skeleton, and large cerebral hemispheres, which were responsible for the senses of vision and co-ordination. The lightness of the skeleton was attained by many of the bones being hollow and air-filled; the skeleton was lent added strength by the fusion of certain parts and the enlargement of some of the structures, such as the sternum, which had to support the wings. The wings themselves were membranous, and supported by the greatly-elongated fourth finger, the remaining fingers being modified into claws. The jaws were still furnished with teeth, and the long tail was adapted to assist balance in flight. Although the earliest Jurassic pterosaurs were not particularly large, some of the later Cretaceous forms attained a wingspan of as much as 27 feet, and had a long, pointed head which looked as though it were too big for the body.

The general skeletal structure of the pterosaurs suggests that they were less active fliers than modern birds, and their aerial movements probably consisted largely of gliding. It seems rather unlikely that they could have walked on land; the large hooked claws of some forms appear to have been adaptations for clinging to trees and rocks. It seems, therefore, fairly certain that these creatures pursued an arboreal existence, but their wings were structurally less efficient than those of either modern birds or bats.

The level of their circulatory development is not certain, and if this was in fact reptilian in type they must have been considerably restricted in their activities. Most fossil pterosaurs occur in marine deposits, indicating that some of them may have been fish-eaters, living among the rocks of the seashore and making periodic forays out to sea for food. A few forms are known from freshwater deposits; these perhaps lived in the trees, and could possibly have been seed or fruit eaters, or insectivorous.

It must, of course, be remembered that the flight mechanisms of the pterosaurs were quite different from those of modern birds. Nothing remotely resembling feathers was present in the pterosaurs, whose wings were more bat-like, being merely membranes stretched taut from the supporting fingers. Their legs must have been quite inadequate for walking, and it seems most probable that, like the bats, the pterosaurs hung suspended upside-down when at rest.

The pterosaurs survived for about 100 million years, becoming extinct at the end of the Mesozoic. Their development had not evolved far enough to enable them to be successful as a group; for all their apparent advantages over their terrestrial contemporaries they were still reptiles, and inevitably were caught up in the drift towards extinction as the Cretaceous drew to a close. Before this occurred, however, they left behind a legacy—a sub-group which eventually was able to survive them and succeed where they had failed. These were the ancestral birds; both these and the pterosaurs had their remote origins in the thecodont reptiles, but it was left to this more progressive sub-group to overcome the handicaps which restricted the pterosaurs and develop into one of the most successful and varied of modern animal classes.

The first true birds

Despite the immense numbers of birds to-day, this group is very poorly represented in the fossil record. The earliest known members of the class appear in the Jurassic, and our only evidence of them is based on two well-preserved skeletons and two isolated feathers (feathers would be very difficult to preserve satisfactorily owing to the absence of bone).

Archaeopteryx, the first true bird, is a hodge-podge of both primitive reptilian characteristics and very advanced avian features. For example, it has feathers, but reptilian teeth. Its feet are bird-like, but its vertebrae and tail are reptilian, and its wings have projecting claws. It has the bone popularly known as the 'wishbone', which is found only in birds, but its brain is reptilian. This mixture of reptilian and avian characteristics gives us the clearest possible indication of the reptilian ancestry of the birds. No fossils of earlier transitional forms have ever been discovered.

Curiously enough, there is a gap of about 50 million years in avian history from the appearance of *Archaeopteryx* in the Jurassic until the Cretaceous, when two later forms appeared. Even more curious is the fact that one of these later forms was flightless, like the modern emu; in fact the flightless birds which flourished during Cenozoic times must have been not unlike our present-day ostriches and their kin in appearance, and seem to have been savage predators and formidable enemies of the mammals which were contemporary with them.

Other Cenozoic birds became adapted to widely different kinds of life, such as the penguins of the Antarctic, the seabirds of the oceans, the waders of the shores and estuaries, the powerful birds of prey, and the more familiar perching birds of the woodland. Their size range was tremendous: the first known humming-bird could have weighed no more than $\frac{1}{10}$ oz, while at the other end of the scale the elephant-bird of Madagascar stood ten feet high!

The Cenozoic era saw also the development of speed in flight, migration, and song. Some birds then, as now, were solitary, while others were gregarious, living in flocks of anything up to a hundred thousand. Judged from any of these standards the birds are one of the most successful of all living groups of animals, and have travelled far from the earthbound reptiles from which they sprang.

Finally, let us now look more closely at some of the essential modifications which enabled the birds to attain such a measure of success.

The temperature of the body is several degrees above that of man. This necessitates a large supply of oxygen, adequate lungs, and an efficient circulatory system in order to maintain it at this level. In the reptiles and amphibians pure and impure blood are not completely separated in the bloodstream, but the birds have evolved a circulatory system as efficient as that of man, with a four-chambered heart and only one main vessel, the aorta, carrying all the oxygenated blood to the body. The evolution of this great advance in the birds took place independently, however, from that in mammals, since while the heart and the aorta in man are situated towards the left side of the body, in birds these organs are on the right side. This parallel evolution is a very frequently-encountered feature of development in the story of living things.

In birds the embryo is still not ready for life in the outside world for some time after the laying of the eggs, and so the eggs must be kept warm for the maintenance of body temperature in the embryo. This therefore necessitates a period of incubation, during which the parent bird sits on the eggs in order to maintain this body temperature. A further development of parental care is necessary after hatching, since most baby birds are naked and helpless, and unable to find food for themselves. Later we shall see when studying the evolution of the mammals how this process has been simplified by the development of the embryo to a more advanced stage before birth, its body temperature being maintained by retention within the body of the parent.

The eyes of birds—even the most modern ones—show a clear relationship with those of their reptilian ancestors. Around the orbit in many primitive vertebrates from the fishes upwards is a circle of bony plates; this was originally for protection from the pressure of the water in which the creatures swam. In the birds this circle of bone is still present, but in a greatly reduced form *within* the eyeball; its function now is against the pressure of the wind during flight. The brain is very much larger than that of reptiles, but the increase in size appears to be related not so much to intelligence as to the development of the centres of the nervous system which control sight, balance and co-ordination.

The main modification in the axial skeleton is the tremendous extension of the sternum, which covers nearly the whole of the underside of the pectoral region and supports the powerful chest muscles which govern flight. The 'wishbone', found only in birds, is modified in other animals to form the clavicle or collar-bone. The original five fingers of the primitive vertebrates, which are retained in many higher vertebrate groups, are in the birds reduced to four, both in the wings and in the feet. While in the fossil birds the other three fingers are reduced to claws which project from the anterior edge of the wings, in modern birds they are fused, reduced and devoid of claws, and act as supplementary supports for the wings.

A further point of interest is that the pelvis in birds is almost identical with the same structure in the ornithischian dinosaurs (hence their name), and the legs of birds and the hind legs of certain dinosaurs are structurally almost exactly similar. The toothless jaws and the horny bill which are characteristic of all modern birds are also found in certain dinosaurs, as well as in some of the flying reptiles which we have discussed earlier. Even flight in itself is not a distinctive avian feature, since, as we have already seen, several of the fossil flying forms were true reptiles, and not birds. The most distinctive physical feature is doubtless the development of feathers, but even this is only a superficial distinction, for the feathers of birds and the horny scales of reptiles are identical in chemical composition.

Many modern animal groups bear the unmistakable imprint of their ancestry. However, it would be true to say that nowhere in the animal kingdom has this been so marked as in the birds, and if only the gaps in the evolutionary history of some other groups could be as easily breached as the great stride forward from the reptile stock to the dominance of the air, then the palaeontologist's work would be greatly simplified.

15

The Concept of Mammals

A great step forward

MEANWHILE, while their contemporaries the birds were taking to
the air, another branch of the reptilian stock was evolving towards a
more highly-specialised adaptation to enable the group as a
whole to colonise the land more successfully than their ancestors,
and to become more independent of the restrictions imposed by
the limitations of reptilian life. At first we might well imagine that
the evolution of such a highly-developed group as the mammals
would have been quite a late development from the stem reptiles,
but, strange as it may seem, the reverse is the case. The reptilian
stem from which the mammals sprang was one of the very first
sub-groups to differentiate from the original primitive reptile stock,
and the first true mammals appeared little later than the first of
the dinosaurs.

In the latter part of the Permian and the early Triassic we find
the first occurrence of mammal-like reptiles, which appear to
have descended from the pelycosaurs. The most well-known of the
early mammal-like reptiles is *Cynognathus* ('dog-jawed'). This
creature was close to the main line of the group's evolution and
already far along towards the true mammalian condition.

Cynognathus was less heavily-built than many of its contemporaries,
and reached about five feet in body length. The skull was intermediate in type between that of a primitive reptile and that of
a mammal; in fact, many of the bones of the head which are absent
in mammals were already greatly reduced or lost. There was
still a pineal opening at the top of the skull, but this, too, was
greatly reduced. The brain was not greatly developed, and was still
more reptilian than mammalian in type. In the jaw the dentary was
by far the largest of all the bones, and in the roof of the mouth
a secondary palate was developed, just as in modern mammals. The
teeth were already differentiated into incisors, canines and molars,

but a similar rate of progress had not yet taken place in the ear, for there was still only a single auditory bone for sound transmission.

The limbs were greatly modified to meet the new conditions now prevailing. They were set further forward in the case of the fore-limbs and further back in the case of the hind limbs, and the bones themselves were greatly modified. Joints which were later to become lost in later types were in *Cynognathus* very small, and the general conformation of the body and limbs gives the impression that the animal was much lighter on its feet and led a more active life than its more orthodox reptilian contemporaries.

Unfortunately we cannot, of course, be certain from the fossil evidence about various features which time would destroy, such as the flesh and other soft parts, whether these creatures had hair or scales, and so on. We are not even sure that they were warm-blooded, or whether they suckled their young. However, the image which emerges from what we *do* know about *Cynognathus* would appear to be that of a transitional type between the true lizards and the mammals, with an oddly dog-like head; although arbitrarily grouped with the reptiles its mammalian affinities were unmistakable.

Soon many more mammal-like reptiles emerged during the later Permian and early Trias. Some were much more mammal-like in appearance than the dog-jawed reptile, and were very common during these times. The group, however, was not destined to survive beyond the Mesozoic, but before gradually becoming extinct it gave rise to the first true mammals, whose first faint traces appear in rocks of late Triassic origin.

The first true mammals which appear to have become established during the late Mesozoic era are poorly known, and a great deal of our so-called knowledge of them is based more on supposition than concrete evidence. During the whole of the Jurassic and Cretaceous periods—estimated at about 60 million years—fossil mammal finds have been fragmentary, and not one complete skeleton of these early forms has yet been found. Not even a complete skull, which would be of inestimable value, has turned up, and what we know of these ancestral types is based almost entirely upon isolated teeth and jaws.

Typical Mesozoic mammals were usually very small—about the size of a large rat—and according to their teeth they must have been flesh-eaters like their reptilian ancestors. Since they were obviously too small to attack larger vertebrates, they probably subsisted on the worms, slugs and insects which by now had become established on Earth. They may also have eaten the eggs of reptiles.

The brain was still very poorly developed in these forms, though much advanced over the reptilian brain. Some features indicate a tree-dwelling existence and, as in the case of many of their modern descendants, they may have been nocturnal. Being so small and inconspicuous must have been a great advantage to them. It must not be overlooked that they existed contemporaneously with the dinosaurs, many of which were carnivorous, and so the threat of a violent death was always close. However, by taking to the trees and hiding among the foliage or in hollow trunks (much as many arboreal mammals do to-day) they were able to escape from their enemies.

The breakthrough to independence

Quite early in their history the true mammals branched into three main groups. The primitive *monotremes,* of which the duck-billed platypus is an example, and the pouched *marsupials* such as the opossum and the kangaroo, will be described in the next chapter; these two groups form a very small proportion of the mammal class. All other living forms belong to the great third division, the *placental mammals,* which are characterised by the development of a structure known as the *placenta,* by which the developing embryo is attached to the wall of the uterus, or womb, and obtains food and oxygen from the mother's body.

To cut a long story short, this method of reproduction results in the birth of young at a much more advanced stage of development than in the marsupials, and this longer gestation period, together with the period of parental care that follows, have contributed to the dominance of the placentals as a group. The additional protection of the young both before and after birth, together with this long developmental period, give rise to the trend of bigger though fewer offspring; quality rather than quantity, as it were, obviated the need for the production of vast quantities of young, since with parental care they would now have a much greater chance of survival than if they were left to fend for themselves. Usually the fewer the number of young, the longer the period of parental care and the greater the chance of survival to the adult stage. For example, in a fish such as the cod, which can lay up to a million eggs, only three or four may eventually reach maturity; while a mammal such as the polar bear, which normally gives birth to only one cub, rarely twins, would very seldom lose the cub or cubs, except perhaps by some accident. The more advanced state of the embryo at birth also enables the young animal to be better equipped to withstand the various conditions into which it is born.

The brain as well as the body is able to benefit from this longer preparation period. The degree of intelligence with which a young animal is already endowed at birth will have a great bearing on its ability to learn from parental example and thus become fitted eventually to take its place in the outside world, able to find its own food, outwit its natural enemies, and hold its own generally against the inexorable conditions of its environment.

Let us now look at some of the various divisions of the placental mammals, and see for ourselves exactly how far they have travelled along the evolutionary road, via the amphibian and reptilian by-pass, from their fishy ancestors.

Insectivorous mammals

As we have seen, the earliest placental mammals were small, and carnivorous, in the broad sense that they were not plant-eaters; this is evident from their dentition. As already mentioned, insects, worms and similar creatures were already inhabiting the earth, and doubtless these formed the main diet of the first mammals. If their skulls—particularly their jaw and teeth characteristics—are compared with those of the modern mole or hedgehog, we shall observe a great number of similar features. Insectivorous mammals of modern times, like their ancient forbears, are still mainly small and inconspicuous, and have retained the same feeding habits to this day; on the whole this is the group which has departed least from the primitive placental stock. Here we have an example of the persistence of a primitive group of animals due to their highly-specialised mode of life and relative isolation.

The shrews, which are perhaps less familiar to us than some of the other families of this group owing to their shy habits and very small size, are probably the most closely-related to their ancient Mesozoic ancestors. The shrews are a very interesting group, and have played a greater part in evolutionary history than one would perhaps imagine from their inconspicuous size. One member of this group is the smallest of all known mammals.

Shrews are incessantly active, and very wary and nervous in disposition. They are practically impossible to tame, and generally extremely difficult to maintain alive in captivity, owing to their need for tremendous quantities of food in relation to their size. Their food, which consists of insects and other small invertebrates, has to be available at all times, as they do not eat at long intervals as most other mammals do. Their small size results in a relatively high heat loss through the skin, to offset which they eat voraciously to maintain their body metabolism.

The tree-shrews of the tropics are especially important as being thought to provide a link with the higher mammals. Although the first placental mammals were most probably arboreal, most modern insectivorous mammals have become terrestrial or even subterranean in their mode of life; but the tree-shrews have remained persistently arboreal.

The carnivorous mammals

The increase in size as the placental mammals developed enabled some of them to enjoy (if that is the right word) larger prey. In order to do this the animal concerned must be able to catch and kill the prey, and therefore, as one may expect, the main line of development in the first carnivores was the improvement of the dental equipment.

The front teeth, or incisors, are needed for biting and tearing, while the canines are longer and more pointed and are used in a stabbing action. Sometimes these teeth are elongated to become tusks, which are formidable weapons of offence and defence. The molars in carnivores are usually furnished with sharp ridges and pointed cusps.

A carnivore must be fast on its feet to catch its prey, and it must be supple and retain its claws in order to attack. The claws are well-developed in all carnivores, and the body is usually stream-lined to give the animal a fast turn of speed. The cheetah is reputedly the fastest mammal on earth, and although the speeds attributed to it vary a great deal according to the authority responsible for the pronouncement, the cheetah can certainly outrun a horse, though it is very doubtful if it can keep ahead of a motor-car, as some highly imaginative persons have averred.

The ungulates or hoofed mammals

In contrast to the carnivores, the *ungulates* or hoofed mammals are all plant-eaters, and some of them, such as various antelopes, form the prey of lions and other carnivores. Let us now look at the story of ungulate evolution.

The main changes from the primitive placental stock are connected with the teeth and the limbs. The sharp-pointed teeth of the ancestral placentals were not needed for a purely vegetable diet, nor could they be used for the protracted chewing of leaves and grass required for the specialised type of digestion in ungulates. The molars have therefore become greatly enlarged, with flattened grinding surfaces, and in many members of this group the molars have become high-crowned, the originally low cusps rising much higher than the roots.

Faster speed is again essential here, this time not to enable the animals to catch prey but to escape from predators. Another reason for well-developed limbs is that many of the ungulate families range over long distances between seasons to find new pastures. An expanse of grass will only support a given number of animals during a limited period, and when the grass has gone the animals must go, too.

In ungulates the limb joints and bones are so constructed as to be extremely efficient for forward motion, though not well adapted for other types of movement. A horse or cow, for example, finds it somewhat difficult to regain its feet after falling in an unaccustomed position on a slippery road or into a ditch.

In fast-running animals the proximal joints of the limbs are short in order to give a fast muscular drive, while the distal joints are much longer and have a greater range of swing. The bones of the feet are elongated to the extent that the animal can literally run on its toes; with the further development of speed, the toes themselves rise until only their tips touch the ground. As a herbivore does not need claws, but these toes require protection from abrasion during active running, hooves have developed for this purpose. Fig. 50 shows some of these limb adaptations.

When the feet are lifted in this way it will be obvious that the shorter side toes which no longer reach the ground will cease

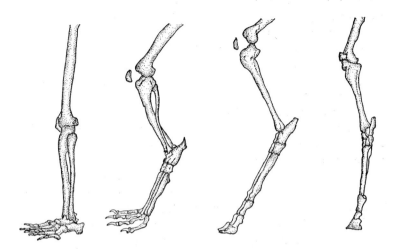

FIG. 50   Some mammalian limb adaptations

to be functional. In this connection two types of development have
taken place: the first is where the axis of the foot lies through the
middle toe, leading to the development of either one-toed animals
such as the horse or three-toed types such as the rhinoceros. The
second direction of development has taken the axis between the
third and fourth toes, leading to the development of the cloven-
hoofed or two-toed types such as cattle, deer and pigs.

We now have another problem to consider. Most small or medium-
sized ungulates can manage very well with the type of foot development we have already described; but in very large and heavy forms
such as the elephants the support of the tremendous weight is of
major importance, and the limbs must be adapted accordingly. We
now have the elongation of the bones in reverse; in the hind limbs
the femur is long while the tibia and fibula are short, with a corresponding elongation of the humerus and truncation of the radius and
ulna in the forelimbs. Both fore and hind limbs are also shorter in
relation to the body, and the feet now have to be very broad so as to
support it. In these types there is therefore no need for a reduction of
the toes; instead they are spread outwards and provided with a

thick pad underneath which unifies the toes into one solid structure.

The earliest ungulates did not appear until Tertiary times. The first ungulate looked rather like the modern tapir, but had a longer tail and shorter limbs. A curious feature was that, while all the toes were still present, each was separately hoofed. The earliest known representative of this group was once believed to be the actual ancestor of many of the later hoofed mammals, but this is not now thought to be the case as it evolved too late in time, being contemporary with the early horses, whose remains were subsequently discovered in the same strata.

In Eocene times more progressive ungulates were already under way. These comprised two groups, the even-toed (or cloven-hoofed) and the odd-toed. We will survey the latter first.

The most important living representatives of the odd-toed ungulates are the horses, the rhinoceroses and the tapirs.

The first horses

The first horse known from the fossil record, *Eohippus* ('dawn horse') appears right at the beginning of the Eocene. This, the first of the true horses, has never failed to capture the imagination of the palaeontologist. It was no bigger than a dog, but was easily recognisable as a horse none the less. Slimly-built, with long legs, the reduction in the number of toes had already begun, although there were still four toes on the front limbs and three on the hind limbs. The molars were still low-crowned, which implies that *Eohippus* was more probably a browser than a grazer. *Eohippus* was not only the first of the long line of horses, but was also probably close to the ancestral stock from which the other odd-toed ungulates have descended.

The subsequent history of the horses can be summarised briefly as involving four main evolutionary developments. These were: an overall increase in size, the lengthening of the limbs and modifications to the feet, various changes in the skull and dentition, and an increase in both the relative size and complexity of the brain.

The general tendency towards an increase in body size was frequent in Cenozoic mammals. Whereas *Eohippus* stood only 12 inches high at the shoulder, the modern horse may be over 5 feet. While such an increase in size confers certain advantages, nevertheless it also presents problems. Without going into the physical principles involved, an increase in height of four times, for example, involves a relative increase in weight of 64 times, but a corresponding increase in the strength of the supporting limbs of only 16 times. We therefore would be quite wrong to visualise a modern horse as being merely a larger edition of *Eohippus,* since such an animal would be physically unfitted for life. What we do find, however, is that the entire body has undergone quite drastic structural adaptations, the trend of which is most obviously observed in the proportions of the limbs and the teeth.

The teeth, however, do not only reflect the general increase in size; their surface area, length (i.e., their durability during life) and efficiency are all involved in the overall change. During Miocene times the changes in vegetation necessitated a radical alteration from the browsing habit to grazing, and therefore the teeth had to undergo a relatively rapid modification at this time to enable the group to survive.

The limbs now had to be adapted to meet the new conditions. A grazing life on open grassland implies a requisite ability to run at a fast speed in order to escape from natural enemies—an ability much less necessary to animals which browse on shrubs and bushes, since they are less visible under the cover of their wooded habitat. This ability was conferred by the gradual reduction in the number of toes, from four in *Eohippus* to three in the Oligocene *Mesohippus,* and subsequently, via a number of less spectacular adaptations, to the one-toed or completely-hoofed form *(Equus)* living to-day.

Mesohippus was not a great deal bigger than its predecessor, but one of the side toes had already been lost and the two remaining lateral toes were already shorter than the main central one. The beginning of the hoof was already in evidence in this latter—a trend which was to be intensified in later forms, such as the Miocene *Parahippus,* in which the teeth were already much longer, suggesting a change of diet from the scrub of forested regions to grass. Another form from this period, *Hipparion,* which survived into the Pliocene, was already the size of a small pony, and was a lightly-built, fast-running type. During the Pliocene period the side toes begin to disappear altogether, and by the beginning of the Ice Age the modern one-toed, completely-hoofed horse *(Equus)* was present all over the world, except Australia.

The rhinoceroses and tapirs

The next group of the odd-toed ungulates is the rhinoceroses, which first appeared in the Eocene and were contemporaries of the early horses; in fact, they looked much more like horses than present-day rhinoceroses, being comparatively small and slender and built to run at a considerable speed. The first rhinoceros had no horns, and to start with the group had all four toes still present on the front feet; it was not until much later that the more heavily-built three-toed rhinoceros evolved.

The group was formerly much more varied and widespread than it is to-day. During Oligocene times the group reached the peak of its development in *Baluchitherium,* which at 18 feet high was the largest land mammal ever to have lived. It was hornless, and the head was shaped more like that of a giraffe than that of its modern descendants. A later type was the woolly rhinoceros, which was a contemporary of early man and lived in Europe during the last glaciation. Two of these curious-looking creatures have been found preserved complete in oil deposits in Galicia, and from these specimens we have been able to find out a great deal about the development of this group.

The tapirs are remarkably similar in structure to their ancestral progenitors. Like the rhinoceros, the tapirs underwent a great reduction during Pliocene times and, whereas formerly they were very widespread, their descendants are now restricted to South and Central America and Malaya.

The extinct odd-toed ungulates

In addition to the three groups of odd-toed ungulates represented by living forms, there were also two extinct groups, both of which reached large proportions. The *titanotheres,* which first appeared in the Eocene and were confined to North America, were somewhat horse-like superficially, but rapidly developed towards a very large size (hence their name) and ponderous build, some of them reaching 8 feet in height at the shoulder. Four toes were retained on the forelimbs and three on the hind limbs throughout their history, and they were slow of speed. They were herbivorous, and apparently were preyed upon by some of the large carnivores of their day, in response to which their need for self-defence was served by paired horns appearing over the nasal region. Following this climax in development both as to size and numbers the group suddenly disappeared, no remains having been discovered in strata of later than Oligocene origin, and it is thought that since their teeth were suitable only for dealing with soft plant food, the rapid climatic upheavals of the time must have caused changes in the vegetation pattern of their territories too quickly to enable the titanotheres to have time to become adapted to a new diet by evolving teeth better equipped to deal with it.

The other group of extinct odd-toed ungulates is the *chalicotheres*, which were later to disappear from the scene than the preceding group. Not uncommon during Tertiary times, in body form they were not unlike horses, but their teeth were identical to those of the titanotheres. Their feet, however, were nothing like those of either; their toes terminated not in hooves but in huge claws. Palaeontologists argued among themselves whether such claw-toed forms could be included in an ungulate group, but eventually it was assumed that the claws were merely an adaptation for digging out the roots and tubers upon which these animals appear to have fed.

The even-toed ungulates

Much more successful have been the even-toed ungulates, which are now the dominant members of the order. They are a relatively recent development, having evolved from an ancestral Eocene stock. The most primitive living members of the group are the pigs and their relatives, some of whose Tertiary forbears were as large as horses.

The even-toed ungulates are adapted to a tremendous variety of habitats, such as the hippopotamus of tropical African rivers, the camel of the desert, the elk and reindeer of the tundra, antelopes and giraffes of the grasslands, wild sheep and goats of mountain regions, and the cattle and bison of the plains. Most of these groups were far more widespread in former times; even during the Pliocene there were wild hippopotami in Britain. The rapid expansion of this group is thought to be a direct result of the development of the ruminant habit of many of their members. In a world peopled by savage carnivores, the ability to eat in haste and digest at leisure—in other words, chewing the cud—confers distinct survival advantages.

For all practical purposes the even-toed ungulates may be divided into the swine, which do not chew the cud, and the ruminants. In the former the four toes are still clearly present, although the side toes are much reduced and the limbs are short: not much speed can be developed. The diet is omnivorous, in contrast to their more advanced ruminant relatives. Living forms include the wild boar, from which the domestic pig is derived, and the wart-hog of Africa. Closely-related to these are the peccaries, small and more lightly-built forms with tusks which grow straight downwards. The hippo-potamus is, of course, a relative of the pig, although its name actually means 'river-horse'. It is found now only in tropical Africa and, unlike other living members of the pig family, it is a river-dweller. The Red River Hog, which I have seen (and eaten) while I was in West Africa, does not live in the water, but is found near streams, where it feeds on roots and tubers, snails and other inverte-brates which it finds in the soft earth.

The pig-like group had many more representatives in Oligocene and Miocene times, the most important of these extinct forms being the giant hogs or *entelodonts,* which were almost as large as a buffalo. Strange as it may seem, the extinct swine were more progressive than their present-day descendants, especially in the matter of their limbs, which were much longer and only two-toed.

The other and much more important division of the even-toed ungulates is the ruminants. The stomach in ruminants is a highly-complicated organ consisting of four separate chambers, and digestion in these animals is a much more complex process than in other mammals. The side toes have tended to disappear fairly rapidly, and living members of the group have only two functional toes, although sometimes the lateral ones are represented by vestigial remnants, comparable to the 'dew claws' of a dog.

There is evidence that a group of primitive ruminants which flourished in the early part of the Tertiary era was ancestral to several groups of later forms, including some offshoots of the original stock. The Oligocene *creodonts,* for example, were a transitional group closely related to modern ruminants when judged by their teeth, but having at the same time many affinities with the swine, such as four-toed limbs and stocky build.

While these primitive ruminants were evolving, the pattern was being laid for the higher groups at quite a rapid rate. The camels and llamas were among the earliest of the higher ruminants to develop, and also the group most distinct from other members of the order.

The feet of camels are adapted to support them in a sandy habitat, while the much smaller llamas, very different in appearance, are adapted to mountain-living. The hump of the camel, which stores body fat and water to tide it over periods of drought, is absent in the llama, which does not need such provision; but these two animals are closely related nevertheless. In the early camels of the Oligocene and Miocene there was no hump; this is because their habitat in those days was grassy plains, and so there was no problem of food or water conservation. As in all grassland animals, their legs were much longer, and side toes were absent.

The deer form a comparatively unprogressive group compared to some of their more advanced relations, having remained primarily browsers of the forests, which would appear to have been the original home of the higher even-toed ungulates. They are essentially animals of temperate regions, some extending into the Arctic, though a few are found in the tropics.

The most obvious feature of deer structure is the development of antlers. It is incorrect to refer to a deer's 'horns', since a true horn, as in the cow, is covered with a hardened type of skin, whose chemical structure is identical with that of our finger-nails. In the deer, however, the antler consists only of bone, without any horny covering. During the growth of young deer the antlers are at first covered by a soft, furry, velvet-like material, but this distintegrates and is rubbed off as growth is completed. Antlers also differ from horns in two other features. Whereas a true horn is a single structure, an antler is divided into a number of branches; a still more important difference is that while a horn is a permanent structure, antlers are shed and renewed every year.

The most primitive members of this group are the chevrotains or water-deer of tropical Africa and south-eastern Asia. These are very tiny animals, one species of which is very little bigger than a large rat. They are devoid of antlers, but some of them have sharp tusks which are used as defensive weapons. A few of them still retain four toes, which are possessed by no other ruminants.

The water-deer are living relics of a group which flourished in Oligocene times and which were almost identical to their modern descendants. They were close to the ancestral ruminant stock which in Oligocene times was already beginning to specialise into various lines of descent. Some of these branches are now extinct, but others

F

have led to the existing families of higher ruminants which we have already described. In most cases there was a tendency towards increase in size and the development of antlers.

The giraffes are the next group which we should briefly survey. They are a further and more advanced group of higher ruminants ('higher' may here be taken literally as well as metaphorically!). The giraffe is a browsing animal inhabiting the savanna lands, and so in a habitat where trees are few and far between it has had to develop a suitable mechanism to make the most use of what is there. The long neck enables it to reach branches inaccessible to other animals, and it has thereby found it possible to avoid competition from its more earthbound relatives.

The long neck of the giraffe is very interesting in that it has not involved the addition of a single vertebra to the axial skeleton. The neck of any mammal contains seven vertebrae; so does that of the giraffe, but each vertebra is greatly elongated. Let us now compare this situation with that in the whale, which has hardly any neck to speak of. Once again we find that the whale has seven cervical vertebrae, but here each one is compressed until it is almost flat. While, as we have seen, reptiles have a tremendous degree of variation in the number of their cervical vertebrae, mammals never deviate from the 'rule of seven'.

The fossil ancestors of the giraffes were similar to living forms in every respect except that they had short necks, and it is interesting to compare the size of the individual cervical vertebrae in the Pliocene giraffe to those in the modern form. The okapi, which was discovered in the Congo in the early part of this century, although so different in appearance from the giraffe, is actually very closely related to it.

The largest group of the higher ruminants is that of the bovines, which include cattle, sheep and goats. Mainly dwellers of the plains, they have, like horses, high-crowned teeth, and subsist mainly upon grass. In almost all members of this group true horns have developed.

The bovines were comparatively late in time to evolve, for there were few of them in the Miocene, and it is only towards the end of the Tertiary that they have become numerous. They are now the dominant hoofed mammals, and in fact outnumber all the other forms. Some of the smaller types living to-day are very similar to their fossil forbears, though they are very different in distribution; the musk oxen, for example, which are now confined to Arctic regions, had a much more southerly distribution during the Ice Age, both in Europe and America. The bison and the buffalo were among the later members of the group to appear.

In contrast to their odd-toed relatives, the even-toed ungulates are a flourishing group. Their success is due perhaps less to their improved dentition and better brains than to their limb adaptations, which were essential for survival, and perhaps even more to the development of the stomach. It is probably a combination of all four of these features which has contributed to their spectacular success.

16

Eternal Childhood

Monotremes, marsupials and neotenic animals

AT THE lowest level of mammal organisation are the *monotremes*, which we shall look at briefly first. These are, one might say, the mammals which did not quite make it—they are so reluctant to relinquish their reptilian family background that they still lay eggs, and their skeleton is more reptilian than mammalian in many ways. Neither do they go all the way in producing milk for their young in well-developed mammary glands like other mammals; modified sweat-glands only are as far as they go, and the 'milk' produced by these is modified, too. The period of lactation is also much shorter than that of 'ordinary' mammals.

Fossil monotremes have not been discovered in deposits of earlier than Pleistocene origin, though it is highly probable that they actually originated much earlier than this. Only two monotremes remain in existence to-day, the duck-billed platypus *(Ornithorhynchus)* and the spiny anteater *(Echidna)* of Australia. These creatures, despite their low level of mammalian organisation, are very highly-specialised to fit them for the particular life they lead.

Both the duck-billed platypus and the spiny anteater are devoid of teeth (although the platypus has a few rudimentary teeth in its early juvenile stage). The platypus is a denizen of the streams and is a very good swimmer, but it is also well-adapted for digging, since it nests in burrows excavated in the banks. The broad horny bill amply compensates for the lack of teeth.

The echidna is protected by a covering of stout spines comparable to those of the hedgehog. Beneath these spines, however, the skin is furry. The echidna feeds exclusively on ants, and in order to do this it is equipped with powerful digging claws with which it rips open the ant-hills. The long, slender snout is also useful in these operations, in particular for getting the long, sticky tongue into the interior of the ant-hills to lick up ants dozens at a time.

It is important to remember that these two curious types have had a separate line of ancestry and are not descended from the progenitors of the higher mammals, which abandoned egg-laying and bore their young alive even in Mesozoic times. It seems, therefore, more than likely that the platypus and the echidna are degenerate forms whose persistence is directly attributable to their isolation on the Australian continent. Nevertheless, geographical reasons alone may not account entirely for an animal's isolation; it may also become isolated by taking up a mode of life in which there are few competitors. The isolation of these two Australian remnants may well be due to both these factors.

The marsupials

The *marsupials* are another very minor group, represented mainly by the kangaroos, wallabies, wombats and koala bears of Australia, the Tasmanian wolf, the opossums of the New World. The marsupials are the *pouched mammals,* whose young are born in a comparatively immature state—little more than animated embryos—which, immediately after birth, climb up into the mother's pouch, where they live a sheltered existence attached to the teats from which they draw their nourishment, remaining there until they have grown and developed sufficiently to venture out into the world.

Many of the skeletal features of living marsupials are primitive, differing little from that of their Upper Cretaceous ancestors. A great many different types of marsupials evolved from these and spread throughout Tertiary times, including large forms as big as tigers. As the more advanced placental mammals colonised the New World the marsupials declined, owing to the fierce competition offered by their more progressive relatives. In Australia, however, the much greater geographical isolation, together with the facility with which this group has been able to adapt to various types of habitat, have tended to provide a more secure environment with far less threat from more advanced competitors, and it is to these factors that kangaroos, wallabies, wombats and their relatives owe their survival.

Neotenic animals

A very few animals have, as it were, given up altogether and have taken refuge from the fierce competition of adult life by retreating into their juvenile world and refusing to emerge as fully-developed adult forms. Imagine a tadpole preferring to remain a tadpole all its life, and never becoming a frog; this is precisely what happens in certain cases, such animals being termed *neotenic*.

The living salamanders and their relatives are not markedly different from their ancient forbears. They exhibit many degenerate features, both in the skull and in the axial skeleton; the group has never travelled very far, evolutionally-speaking, along the road to progress. They are typical amphibians in that their skin is soft and moist and plays a vital part in their respiratory system: salamanders cannot survive in dry conditions, and when not actually in the water they will ensconce themselves in some moist microhabitat such as under a rotting log.

The axolotl *(Amblystoma)* of Mexico and adjoining territories, an inhabitant of ponds and lakes, is a neotenic type which breathes through gills and remains a juvenile or larval form all its life, just so long as the water of its habitat does not dry up. Should this occur in time of drought, a very curious thing happens. The axolotl, which may well have been an axolotl for several years, now gradually metamorphoses into a black-and-orange spotted salamander, losing its gills and emerging complete with functional lungs. The adult salamander lives on land—albeit in a moist type of habitat as with all amphibians—and only returns to the water to breed.

Even more curious, however, is the fact that *the axolotl can breed in the immature state*. A juvenile or larval form that is sexually mature to the extent that it is capable of reproducing its kind is a phenomenon indeed—an example of neoteny carried to extremes!

If you keep an axolotl in an ordinary aquarium, it will remain an axolotl, and if you have a male and a female they will produce eggs which will hatch into more axolotls. Now gradually reduce the level of the water in the aquarium, providing a bank of earth at one end of the tank. As the water-level drops and the axolotls are forced to come out more and more on to the 'land', metamorphosis will gradually ensue, and your pair of axolotls will become a pair of salamanders. When your salamanders' breeding season approaches they will need water in which to lay their eggs, which will, of course, hatch into baby axolotls and not little salamanders (any more than frog spawn would hatch into baby frogs without passing through the tadpole stage).

Another way in which the axolotl can be induced to metamorphose is by feeding or injecting it with thyroid extract, which is quite a simple procedure to carry out in the laboratory.

The Peter Pan of the animal world

Another example of a neotenic animal is the mud-puppy, which is found in the western United States and looks rather like an axolotl with a distinctly dog-like face (shades of *Cynognathus!*). The mud-puppy's lungs remain permanently undeveloped, and so it has no choice but to remain in the water and breathe through gills all its life.

Biologists have not, however, succeeded in inducing the American mud-puppy to 'grow up', either by means of thyroid treatment, the gradual reduction of the water-level, or any other means. The mud-puppy can truly be called the Peter Pan of the animal world.

You may now be tempted to wonder whether there are actually any animals which start at the top instead of at the bottom and working their way up, as it were—in other words, animals which start life as adults and skip the juvenile stage altogether. The answer to this, surprisingly enough, is yes indeed—at least three species of animals give birth to comparatively large and well-developed replicas of themselves (neoteny in reverse!). You will hardly be surprised, I am sure, to know that these three animals are all species of salamanders! Nature has certainly singled out this group to demonstrate some of her greatest apparent inconsistencies.

17.

The Stage is set for Man

The first primates

THE earliest known primates were the *lemuroids,* which first appeared just before the beginning of the Eocene and were arboreal, lemur-like creatures, which most probably descended from tree-dwelling primitive placental mammals not unlike the living tree-shrews. The living lemurs and bushbabies are archaic remnants of this early group. Superficially they do not resemble the anthropoid apes and monkeys, but they are distantly related to them via an intermediate linking group, the *tarsioids,* about which we shall say more presently.

The evolutionary documentation of the primates presents quite a problem to the palaeontologist. Whereas in the case of horses, dogs, etc., the fossil history is adequate to enable us to form a reasonably accurate assessment of their development through time, unfortunately fossil remains of primates are rarer than those of any other mammal group. The reason for this is fairly obvious when one realises that primates are mainly tree-dwellers, and that the type of rock deposits in which fossil vertebrates are most likely to be found are not normally formed in forested regions. Secondly, most primates are inhabitants of the tropics, whereas most of the known Tertiary fossil beds are in temperate zones.

Primates are essentially arboreal, only man and the baboons having taken up a terrestrial existence. However, the adaptations which enabled other primate groups to live in the trees are the very developments which have enabled the higher forms to reach their peak. For example, animals living in the trees must have great flexibility of body and be able to grasp the branches with their limbs: there is none of the restriction of limb movement to one plane found in ungulates. The ability to use our hands has therefore been a direct result of the adaptation of the primate limb for grasping. The claws of the more primitive lower forms have been modified into flat finger-nails, which serve to protect the ends of the digits from injury, and the larger space between the thumb and first finger is a specific mechanism for grasping. Since man has adopted a bipedal gait the grasping ability of the big toe is much less necessary to him than, for example, to the orang-utan, which swings from bough to bough. Even in some arboreal forms there is a frequent tendency to sit up on the haunches and eat food with the hands, as opposed to the direct intake of food into the mouth without the assistance of the forelimbs, as in horses and other animals. The primitive long tail which is required to assist in balance in arboreal forms has progressively become reduced until it is absent in terrestrial types.

The dentition is one of the most characteristic primate features. The early primates were omnivorous, and similar feeding habits characterise many of the living forms, although there is a strong tendency in many groups towards a vegetarian diet. The dentition is therefore less specialised than in many other animal groups; the molars are low-crowned, and the excrescences of cusped teeth are rounded. In all primates, including man, the number of incisors has been reduced from the original three to two in each half of each jaw, and there has also been a trend towards the reduction in the number of pre-molars. The higher monkeys and man have 32 teeth, instead of the 44 which were possessed by our primitive placental ancestors. Primates are generally short of jaw, and therefore shorter in the face than most other animals, and only the canine teeth are specialised for biting. In man these teeth do not project above the level of the other teeth in the jaw.

For locomotion in the trees good eyesight is essential; the more so if the animal is nocturnal. Even in the lemurs the eyes are large, but in the galagoes (bushbabies) and tarsioids they are so well-developed as to occupy more of the facial aspect than in any other living creatures.

In vertebrates below the level of the mammals the eyes appear to supply the brain with two separate visual images, but in the higher mammals the visual fields overlap, giving rise to the stereoscopic type of vision which is well-developed in the higher primates. In this type of vision the nerves which run from the eyes to the brain sort out the images so that the brain-pictures formed by the eyes coincide; the minute variation between these two images imparts the effect of depth, rather like the rangefinder in a camera. With improved vision the sense of smell is generally less acute, and even in the lemurs the olfactory organs are greatly reduced, while in the man-like apes and man the sense of smell is the least well-developed of any terrestrial placental type.

Whereas the tree-dweller requires great acuity of vision, the ground-dweller, though of course dependent on vision to a great extent, does not need such precise visual equipment as a mammal which needs to spot its food from several feet up, and to gauge the precise point at which to land from a leap, when missing a branch by a couple of inches might make all the difference between life and death. On the other hand, a terrestrial mammal is much more dependent on smell, for it frequently needs to sniff out the presence of food or an enemy, and so the nostrils are more highly-developed in those mammals which seek their food close to the ground, such as the baboons. Man has become less dependent on his sense of smell during the passage of time, owing to his upright posture.

The brain is the area in which the development of the primates has been most marked. Locomotion in the trees requires great agility and muscular co-ordination, and it must not be overlooked that many of our higher mental faculties are developed in an area which lies immediately adjacent to the locomotor centres of the brain. The brain size has increased throughout the evolutionary history of the higher primates, especially in the region of the cerebral hemi-spheres, which in all the highest anthropoids completely cover the cerebellum. The relative weight of the brain to the body is higher in the anthropoids than in any other placentals.

These changes in the brain, sensory organs and dentition have necessitated far-reaching alterations in the conformation of the head in primates. The lemurs, at the lower end of the scale, have an elongated skull of primitive appearance, with a low cranium and elongated facial characteristics. With the reduction in the teeth and the olfactory organs in the higher forms, the jaws have been con-siderably shortened and the facial area reduced; conversely, the cranium has had to be greatly expanded in order to accommodate the larger brain. In primitive mammals there was no bone separating the eye-sockets from the temporal region, but from the outset the primates had already acquired this separation. While in the earliest forms this structure is somewhat flimsy in conformation, in man and the anthropoid apes and the more advanced monkeys it has become a solid partition between the eyes and the temporal region. No other living animals have this particular feature.

The most primitive primates

The lemurs to-day are restricted to a few localities only, mainly Madagascar. The eyes are situated more laterally than forward, and the ears are more pointed, which gives the face a somewhat fox-like appearance. Despite the arboreal habitat of the lemurs, the long tail is never used as a grasping organ. The space between the thumb and the four fingers is well-developed on each limb; the big toe on the hind limb is especially well-developed and has a flat nail, the other digits being variable according to species.

The isolation caused by the separation of Madagascar from the African mainland has tended to preserve the survival of these primitive forms, since few carnivorous predators have been able to colonise this region; on the mainland lemurs are extremely rare. Their nearest relatives are the lorises, the galagoes or bushbabies, and the potto, all denizens of tropical forest and all somewhat more advanced forms than the typical lemur.

In Eocene times lemurs very similar to living forms were commonly found in Europe and North America, but at the close of the Eocene they vanished from the fossil record of these more temperate regions. The lemurs are exceedingly primitive primates and not far removed from the ancestral tree-shrew types from which the primates appear to have arisen.

The unlikely link

The *tarsioids*, which on all the available evidence would seem to link the lower primates with the anthropoids or man-like group, are small nocturnal tree-dwellers, found only in the East Indies. Curiously intermediate between lemur and monkey, the tarsioids have peculiar rat-like tails and long hind legs, but their brain is large and enclosed in a rounded cranium. Their visual apparatus is greatly advanced over that of the lemurs, the eyes themselves being exceptionally large and brought forward from the more primitive lateral position, with the orbits close together above the nose. Recent research work on the tarsioids indicates that stereoscopic vision is well-developed in these animals.

With the advance in vision, the sense of smell has been proportionately reduced, and the dentition also is of a more advanced type. A most interesting feature of the tarsioids, demonstrating their indisputable affinities with the highest primates, is that in the embryo the placenta connecting the embryo to the mother is no longer, as in the lemurs, distributed all round the amniotic sac, but is concentrated in one area and shed after birth, just as in man and monkeys.

The tarsioids are not monkeys, but they are far above the level of the lemurs. Their first appearance was in Eocene times and so they were contemporaries of the early lemurs, which would appear to indicate that, although they would seem to bridge the gap between the lemurs and the anthropoids, they did not actually descend from the lemurs, but stemmed directly from the ancestral tree-shrews.

The monkeys

An important advance in eye structure separates the monkeys from all lower forms, and marks a great advance in visual acuity which is continued in ourselves. A small area in the centre of the eye, known as the *fovea centralis,* ensures clear perception of detail; this unique feature, already present in the lowest of the monkeys, is not found in any other animals.

The greatly-enlarged brain-case required to house the much bigger brain gives the skull a much more human shape. Although normally a four-footed walker, there is an increasing tendency towards the upright sitting posture, as well as the use of the hands for feeding and investigation of objects which is continued in the higher forms, eventually resulting in great manual dexterity.

The New World or American monkeys are easily recognisable from their Old World relatives by their more widely-separated nostrils, and also by the fact that there are *three* pre-molar teeth in each half of each jaw, whereas there are only *two* in the Old World types. The smallest of all monkeys are the marmosets, which are members of this New World group. Much more typical are the capuchin monkeys, which have long prehensile tails and are very clever acrobats. Another family of New World monkeys is that of the howler monkeys, whose voice is tremendously amplified (as the zoo visitor soon finds out!) by the large resonating chamber in the throat.

The fossil history of these American monkeys is not very well-known, and they are certainly on a lower level of development than the Old World forms. There is little to indicate that this group lies on the main line of descent of the higher primates, or even close to it.

The Old World monkeys have the nostrils closer together, and are generally much larger in body size. Although primarily four-footed in gait, many of them can walk on the hind legs with the body held more or less erect, and when not in motion usually sit upright. The hairy covering of the body is always much more sparse than that of the thick, furry New World types, and the face is always naked.

The brain is larger in this group than in the New World monkeys, and there is also an increase in the size of the teeth, although their number has been reduced: they, like man, have 32 teeth.

The anthropoid apes

The anthropoid (man-like) apes date back to the beginning of the Oligocene, and include a number of different types with a wide range of habitat and structure.

Our own line of descent came from a third branch of the primate family tree, diverging from that which led to the anthropoid apes at an earlier date. We shall discuss the evolutionary history of man in more detail in the final chapter, confining ourselves here to the anthropoid apes, which include four living types: the gorilla, the chimpanzee, the orang-utan and the gibbon. The gibbons are not very large, but at the other end of the scale a fully-grown male gorilla may weigh several times more than a man.

In the anthropoids the skeleton is basically not unlike the human type, but the arms are greatly elongated and the legs proportionately much shorter. The feet are still specialised for grasping, with long toes and the big toe opposite to the others in the same way as the thumb and fingers of the hand. The chest is much broader, and its great resonance enables the gorilla and other large anthropoids to make much louder sounds than their smaller-built relatives.

With increasing weight and bulk it became much more difficult for a four-footed animal to run along the branch of a tree. The weight could be more evenly distributed by resting the hind limbs on one branch and grasping an overhanging one with the arms. From this developed the typical swinging movements of the apes, and in fact the hind feet are so specifically adapted to the grasping function that most great apes cannot walk flat on their soles, but must support the weight of the body by walking on the outer sides of the feet.

When swinging the arms the body is naturally held erect, and since the front limbs of all these apes are so much longer than the hind limbs, the body is necessarily more inclined upwards even when walking on all fours. The erect posture, which is essentially a human characteristic, therefore has its origins in the tree-dwelling types.

In the gorilla the growth of the brain has not kept up, as it were, in proportion to the increase in body size, and is relatively much smaller in proportion to the body than it is in other anthropoids. This is what gives the gorilla its ferocious appearance, owing to the low forehead and jutting brows, and it is even more emphasised by the receding chin. The canine teeth are very prominent, and the molars are heavy and elongated in form, which makes the face project more from the head.

The gibbons are the most primitive of the anthropoids, and the largest species, the hoolock gibbon, does not exceed three feet or so in a standing position. These small apes frequently walk on two legs while on the ground, using their very long arms as balancers. However, they do not spend much time on the ground, preferring to show off their arboreal acrobatics. The brain has a capacity of only about 90 cc, making the gibbons the least intelligent of the higher apes. The first gibbons, which occurred in the Tertiary, were very similar to present-day forms.

The next highest in the scale of the anthropoids is the orang-utan, a word which means 'wild man' in one of the Borneo native dialects. An adult male can reach five feet in height, and its brain capacity is more than five times greater than that of the gibbon. There is no development of heavy brow ridges, and therefore the orang-utan is much less fierce in appearance than the gorilla; however, the eyes are set more closely together than in other apes, and the nasal region is more deeply concave, making the facial appearance quite unlike that of other anthropoids.

The highest man-like apes are the chimpanzee and the gorilla. These forms first appeared in Miocene times, and they instigated the first traces of the descent from the tree-tops to the ground. The chimpanzee and the gorilla have not taken this process of terrestrial adaptation very far; it was left to man to make a success of it.

The brain is comparatively well-developed in these great apes. Considerable experimental work has been done in recent years by psychologists in testing the intelligence of these apes, especially the chimpanzee. Memory is well-developed, and there is at least the beginning of reasoning powers of human type.

What does the fossil record show us in the way of ape evolution? Fragmentary remains of large, ape-like primates occur in Miocene and Pliocene deposits in the Old World, mainly in India. It is disappointing that most of these finds have consisted almost entirely of teeth and jaws alone, but since these are among the most characteristic parts of any animal and can tell us much more about its habits than many other parts of the body, a great deal has been learned even from these fragmentary remains.

One thing we do know about these fragmentary teeth and jaws, which have been very carefully studied, is that all possess features found to-day only in three primates—the gorilla, the chimpanzee and man. Some of them possess characteristics implying that they may have been ancestral to the gorilla or the chimpanzee; their features show the beginnings of tendencies which could possibly have led in a human direction, but beyond this statement we cannot go. It is impossible to say that any known fossil anthropoid from this period represents the man-like primate which was actually ancestral to the first true man.

A number of fossil apes discovered recently in South Africa are very interesting, but since they date from the Pleistocene they are too late in time to be considered as actual human ancestors. These apes, however, approach man much more closely in several respects than any other apes, either living or fossil forms.

The first of these to be discovered was a skull, to which the name *Australopithecus* ('southern ape') was given. Part of the cranium had been lost, but this was, curiously enough, more of an advantage than otherwise, because its removal had exposed a perfect cast of almost the entire brain. The individual was a juvenile; this much can be told from the teeth, which correspond to those of a child of about seven years of age.

In some ways the extreme youth of this ape was rather unfortunate, because the differences between a young ape and a child are much less marked than those between adults. The brain size alone, compared on this basis, indicated that the creature was certainly far below the human standard, but on the other hand the skull differed markedly from that of a chimpanzee or gorilla of similar age; the teeth, in particular, showed many human characteristics. It is therefore considered that *Australopithecus* is a very advanced type of ape approaching the human level, though falling a good deal short of reaching it.

Later adult skulls were discovered from other parts of South Africa. Although differing in some details from the first find, and therefore having been given different names, they appear to be fairly closely related to *Australopithecus*. The later finds were also incomplete, but enough of their structure was still intact to enable palaeontologists working on them to restore them. The contours of these adult skulls are still ape-like rather than man-like, the face in lateral view having the concave ape profile without the projecting human nasal structure. However, the brain capacity was estimated in two of the specimens at 450 cc and 650 cc respectively; the latter figure exceeds the largest brain capacity of any known ape.

Strong evidence is forthcoming in the dentition to indicate a fairly close approach to the human type. In apes the teeth are arranged to form three sides of an oblong, the molars forming the two parallel rows, while the projecting canines form the angles at the front. In man the canines do not project, and the whole row of teeth forms a horseshoe-shaped curve. In these fossil skulls the tooth row is curved and the canines are nearly as small as those in man. Furthermore, several of these fossil teeth, including their cusp patterns, are extremely close to the human type.

As we have already pointed out, these 'southern apes' were most probably contemporaries of the first true man, and therefore cannot be his actual ancestors. They apparently represent a structural stage preceding that which led to the development of man, and may possibly be the somewhat unprogressive descendants of the original human stock.

Before we can trace man's evolutionary history, first we must look more closely at some of our physical characteristics to determine the essential features which differentiate them from those of the lower primate branches, and this we shall attempt to do in the next chapter.

18

Man, the Ultimate

What is man?

THE scientific name of man is *Homo sapiens*, which means 'thinking man', and it is this definition—the power of thought and reason—which raises the human race above the level of all other anthropoids. However, before the brain could develop to this tremendous extent, the body had to prepare the way for it; and so first we shall look at the physical features which have played such a vital role in conditioning the setting for this great advance.

The differences between the great apes and modern man seem to us to be extreme, but from a purely anatomical point of view these differences are far less great than they appear to be. The bones, the muscles and the internal organs are almost identical in their actual physical structure; the differences are in their proportions and in their relationship to other parts of the body.

The biggest group of differences are those relating to locomotor and cerebral functions. Among the higher apes we see already the trend towards an erect posture and a terrestrial life, but only man has carried these tendencies to their ultimate conclusion and abandoned the tree-tops and the use of the forelimbs in walking. The arms are no longer needed for swinging in the branches, so they have become shorter; in fact, it is highly improbable that we have descended from any long-armed form. Our arms have always had, as far as we can tell, the shorter proportions seen in those of the lower primates, while the great apes, which have taken to the trees, have always tended towards having long arms but short legs. The human hand, apart from its much greater flexibility, is of the primitive primate type, whereas the hand of the great apes has much longer fingers, an adaptation for hooking them over branches. Little boys who climb trees not infrequently fall, because their hands and feet, for all their flexibility, are not really primarily adapted to this particular form of activity; but whoever saw an ape fall out of a tree? Another reason is that muscular co-ordination is much more highly-developed in the apes to enable them to judge the distance required for a leap, whereas our muscular co-ordination, although well-developed, is employed for other purposes connected with our terrestrial adaptations.

The feet show even greater differences. In primates generally the foot, like the hand, is an efficient grasping structure, but whereas this has been developed to a much greater extent in the arboreal primates such as the great apes, it is practically useless for a ground-living primate, in particular for one whose posterior limbs must support the weight of the whole body owing to an upright walking habit. In man, therefore, the toes have shortened, the big toe having been brought into line with the others, and the heel bone is expanded to form a kind of prop at the back of the foot, this latter being a feature only partly-developed in the great apes. In the evolution of an erect posture the vertebral column has become more curved, resulting in the head and chest regions being directly above the pelvis, which centres the body weight over the legs; if this were not so we should be unable to walk upright.

We have already discussed the differences in dentition; let us now look at the brain. In modern human races the average brain capacity ranges from about 1200 cc to 1500 cc, which is about two to three times greater than that of the great apes. Such a large brain needs corresponding changes in the general appearance of the head and face, the reduction of heavy brow ridges and the development of a higher forehead.

Most palaeontologists define man as a creature able to employ other aspects of nature in his behalf, such as the kindling of fire, the making of tools and weapons from flints, and so on. Many of the early fossil hominids are therefore held to be advanced anthropoid apes if their finding is unaccompanied by the finding of any evidence pointing to the possible use of tools or fire, or something of this kind. On the other hand, early hominids discovered in China and known as Pekin man *(Pithecanthropus)* were found associated with shaped tools made of quartz and bone, and also the charred remains of deer. Some *Pithecanthropus* skulls were also discovered which had been broken in such a way as to suggest that the brain had been removed; this clearly points to *Pithecanthropus* having been a cannibal as well as a hunter of deer and a craftsman already familiar with cooking.

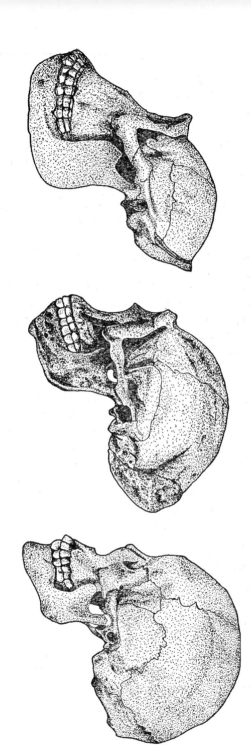

FIG. 51 Skulls for comparison: (a) gorilla, (b) *Pithecanthropus*, (c) modern man

Pithecanthropus was rather squat in build, about five feet in height, with heavy brow ridges, a receding forehead and very powerful jaws, but on the available evidence he also had an erect gait, and both the form and arrangement of his teeth were human. His brain capacity was about 1000 cc which, while being about double that of the largest known living apes, is considerably less than that of modern man. A related species, known as Java man from having been discovered there, had a smaller brain capacity—about 850 cc—while some of the Pekin men had brain capacities of up to 1300 cc, showing that even in those far-off days there was considerable individual variation in the same species. Fig. 51 shows the skull of *Pithecanthropus* and the skull of the gorilla, with a skull of modern man for comparison.

Pithecanthropus is thought to represent the earliest-known true man, for all that he was of low intelligence, savage and cannibalistic, and ape-like in facial appearance (the name *Pithecanthropus* means 'ape-man'). He existed during the early and middle Pleistocene, about half a million years ago and, while it cannot be proved that he was ancestral to the genus *Homo,* he could in many ways have been close to the line of descent.

Early hominids are rare as fossils, and therefore great obstacles are placed in the palaeontologist's way when he tries to put the human family tree into any degree of perspective. Much more commonly found, although never abundant, are the remains of more recent human types. Once man had become a toolmaker it was easier to make deductions, and of course the tools are much more frequently found than the remains of those who used them, since flints and stones are much more resistant to erosion than bones.

The Pleistocene era began about a million years ago, and was represented by a succession of glacial and inter-glacial periods in the northern hemisphere and alternating periods of great floods and droughts in the southern hemisphere. Northern early man had to eke out a precarious existence in Arctic conditions, using the hide of the woolly rhinoceros and the mammoth for protection from sub-zero temperatures, and their meat for his food. His enemies were many and varied, and included the sabre-toothed tiger and other savage predators.

At first man would have just picked up various stones as they lay to hand to use as weapons of offence and defence; it was only later that crude chipping was used as a method of improving their efficacy. Throughout the Pleistocene the variety of tools and the skill and degree of workmanship show a steady increase, and we usually divide this period into two cultural stages, the *Palaeolithic*, up to about 7000 years ago, in which chipping only was employed, after which time the practice of grinding and polishing stone tools gradually became widespread, and this period is therefore known as the *Neolithic*.

What were these first Stone Age men like? With the exception of *Pithecanthropus*, all of them are assigned to our own genus, *Homo*, which is a measure of their resemblance to more modern types. Most of their remains have been found in Europe, the most intelligent being Heidelberg man, first discovered in 1907 and known only from a single lower jaw. Although no tools were found in association with Heidelberg man, fossil animals accompanying his remains suggest that he lived during the first inter-glacial period about half a million years ago. The powerful jaw shows that Heidelberg man had a receding chin and rather heavy facial contours, although his teeth are completely human in character.

Another important find was that of Neanderthal man, also discovered in Germany, and consisting of a skull-cap and limb fragments. This find was much more complete than those of some other types, and Neanderthal man is thought to represent a race similar to, though distinct from, modern man. He lived during the last glaciation and ranged over Europe, northern Asia and North Africa. Other fossil remains from Croatia, Rhodesia and Java show a close resemblance to Neanderthal man, though there are certain differences. All these men had massive brow ridges, a receding forehead and a heavy and prominent lower jaw, features which must have combined to impart a very brutish appearance. This was emphasised by their stooping posture, the short, stockily-built and heavily-muscled body, and slouching gait; yet despite all this their average brain capacity was comparable to that of modern man.

Formerly Neanderthal man was regarded as the ancestor of *Homo sapiens*, but it has now been realised that he was much too late in time to have occupied this position. He is probably a distinct branch of the same genus—he is known scientifically as *Homo neanderthalensis* —running parallel to *Homo sapiens* and sharing a common ancestor with him.

We know a good deal about the life of our Neanderthal relatives during their struggle with the hostile environment of the Ice Age. Their tools included hand axes, scrapers, points and knives, and they were familiar with the use of fire. Most were cave-dwellers and hunted a number of different animals, including the woolly mammoth and rhinoceros; at least some of them appear to have been cannibals.

Beginnings of thought were evident here, however, including the concept of storage of materials which had been found in caves, and the burial of their dead, who had various weapons buried with them. This leaves little doubt that the Neanderthal people had at least some measure of hope of, or belief in, survival after death.

About 30,000 years ago or so, Neanderthal man became extinct, his disappearance having probably been a direct result of the increasing rigours of life in the frozen wastes of the Pleistocene world. However, it is not unlikely that increasing competition from our own species, who had by this time appeared on the scene, was also a contributing factor. Whatever the cause, one thing is certain: *Homo sapiens* was now well-established in Europe and already beginning to spread from there across the rest of the world.

The advent of modern man

Two fossil fragments from Kent are associated with the second inter-glacial period, and are accompanied by implements of comparatively advanced type. The bones themselves show a very strong similarity to those of modern man, and the age of the deposits in which they were found indicates that *Homo sapiens* may possibly have existed for at least 200,000 years. Another more complete fossil from Germany of comparable age has a smaller brain capacity and more prominent brow ridges, but despite this it is generally regarded as a primitive member of our own species.

The next member of our race to appear on the horizon was Cro-Magnon man. Unlike his Neanderthal relatives, he was tall and well-built, with a large brain and facial features very little different from those of modern races. He competed with Neanderthal man in the desolate frozen wastes of the late Pleistocene, but his tools were far superior. He used ivory and bone as well as stone, and had so far advanced as to introduce the first crude bow and arrow, so his competition with the Neanderthals was at an advantage.

Culturally Cro-Magnon man was far advanced beyond the Neanderthal level. Cave paintings of great beauty have been discovered, together with exquisitely-carved and painted figures made from bone. His dead were buried with ceremony, the bodies frequently being adorned with necklaces made of shells coloured with a dye made from plants. A tomb has been discovered in which twenty bodies were laid out, surrounded by the bones of mammoths carefully arranged in patterns around them.

With the advent of Cro-Magnon man we reach a great landmark in our history, for here is the end of the evolution of man as an animal and the dawn of man as a thinking being, capable of worship, artistic thought and conscious rationalisation. Later his cultural advance was to lead along the paths of community and social structure, the development of articulate language, the establishment of traditions, and the working of bronze, iron and other metals. These developments, of course, belong properly to anthropology and archaeology rather than palaeontology, but the relationship between these two aspects of the human race cannot be overlooked, since all these things have been a direct end-product of the growth and complexity of the brain.

Down the long corridors of time the processes of evolution have gone on unceasingly, inexorably, their beginnings so incredibly remote as to defy imagination. The mind boggles at the concept of hundreds of millions of years; but it has taken all this time, and more, to bring us to our final capacity for life at its highest level, with all our powers of reasoning, our skill at adapting our environment to meet our needs, and our feeling for the finer facets of our existence on this planet. The journey along the passage of time, with all its intricate by-ways, from our first remote ancestors as they struggled from the receding waters on to the Triassic mud, has indeed been a long one.

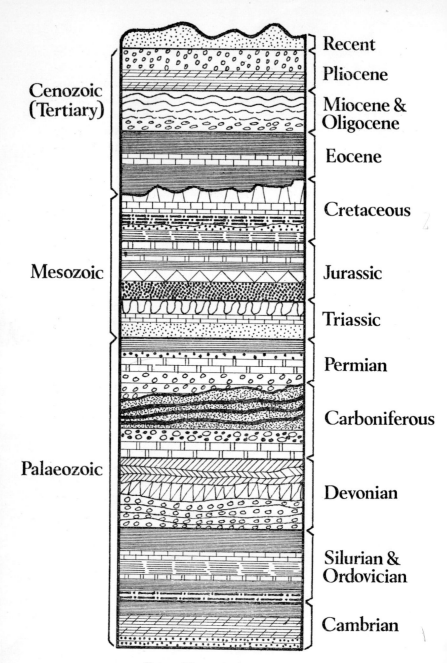

FIG. 52 The geological time-scale

Glossary

Abdomen: the lower part of the body containing the viscera

Abyssal: living in the lowest ocean depths

Acuminate: pointed

Adaptive radiation: evolutional divergence (q.v.)

Agnathous: without jaws

Algae: low forms of plant life, including the seaweeds, *Spirogyra*, etc.

Allantois: a mechanism for supplying oxygen and removing carbon dioxide from a developing embryo

Ambulacral system: the water vascular system in asteroids

Ambulacral tube-feet: the sucker-like feet on the underside of asteroids

Amino-acid: one of the organic constituents of protein

Amnion: a membranous sac containing the amniotic fluid

Amniote: an animal whose developing embryo is surrounded by fluid for shock-absorption

Amniotic fluid: the fluid surrounding the developing embryo to protect it from injury

Amoeba: a typical one-celled animal or protozoan

Amoeboid: moving like an amoeba

Amorphous: devoid of any fixed shape

Amphistylic: the mode of jaw suspension in which the palato-quadrate articulates with the bones of the skull

Anal fin: the fin near the anus in fishes

Analogous (of structures): similar in function, though not necessarily similar in form

Anchylosed: fused to the bone

Anthropoid: man-like

Anus: the rear opening of the digestive tract from which waste is excreted

Aorta: the main vessel of the heart

Aphetohyoid: 'free hyoid', the most primitive type of jaw suspension

Apical disc: a single or double row of plates at the summit of the test in echinoids

Aqueferous system: the system of canals distributing water into, through and out of the body in some lower animal groups

Aqueous: watery

Arboreal: living in the trees

Arthropod: a member of the phylum of jointed-legged animals comprising insects, crustaceans, etc.

Articulated: jointed

Asteroids: the starfishes

Asymmetrical: not equal on both sides

Atoll: a ring-shaped coral reef completely enclosing a lagoon

Atrium: a primitive form of cloaca

Attenuated: drawn out, elongated

Auditory: appertaining to the ear

Autostylic: the mode of jaw suspension in the higher animals, including man

Avian: appertaining to birds

Axial: appertaining to the main stem

Axial skeleton: the main supporting axis of the skeleton, or vertebral column

Barbados earth: polycystine marl deposits of Miocene origin

Basal: appertaining to the base, fundamental

Batrachians: another name for amphibians

Benthos: the sea bottom

Bilaterally symmetrical: the same on both sides

Bilobate: divided into two lobes

Binary fission: the simplest form of reproduction, by splitting into two

Bipedal: walking on two legs

Bovine: appertaining to the ox

Brachial: pertaining to the forelimb or arm

Branchiae: gills

Branchial arches: gill arches

Buccal cavity: the interior of the mouth

Buccal orifice: the mouth

Caecilians: an obscure group of rare burrowing worm-like amphibians found in the tropics

Calcareous: formed from lime or chalk

Calcicole: a plant growing on chalky soil

Calcifuge: a plant unable to grow on chalky soil

Calyx: the 'head' of a crinoid

Canopy: the uppermost woodland layer; the tree-tops

Carapace: protective shield

Carbohydrates: starches

Carnivorous: feeding on other animals

Catalyst: a substance causing chemical changes in other substances but remaining itself unchanged

Caudal: appertaining to the tail

Caudal shield: plate, scute or similar protective covering at the tail end of the body; the pygidium (q.v.)

Centra: the ring-like individual bones of the vertebral column surrounding the spinal cord

Cephalic: appertaining to the head

Cephalothorax: upper part of body in which head and thorax are united

Ceratotrichia: the horny fin-rays in fishes

Cerebellum: the hind-brain

Cerebral: appertaining to the brain

Cerebral hemispheres: the two halves of the brain

Cervical: appertaining to the neck

Chelicerae: jaws, especially in arthropods

Chelonian: appertaining to tortoises and turtles

Chitin: the hard, horny outer covering found in many lower animals

Chlorophyll: the green colouring matter in plants

Choanae: the internal openings to the nostrils

Chondrichthyoids: cartilaginous fishes, e.g. sharks, dogfishes and rays

Chondrocranium: the part of the skull first formed in the vertebrate embryo

Chordate: animal possessing a notochord, a dorsal nerve system and gill-slits at some or all stages of its existence

Chorion: membrane surrounding the amnion to prevent desiccation of the developing embryo

Cilia: whip-like or thread-like extensions of protoplasm

Ciliated: possessing cilia

Cloaca: the common orifice for the expulsion of reproductive and waste products in the lower animals

Coal Measures: another name for carboniferous deposits of Mesozoic origin

Coelenterates: the phylum of animals composed of two layers of cells, e.g. jellyfishes, *Hydra,* etc.

Coelom: the hollow body cavity in coelenterates

Coenosarc: the common stem uniting individual polyps of a colonial coelenterate

Coenosteum: the calcareous skeleton in hydrocorallines

Colloidal: a viscous or gelatinous form of a substance

Colonial: living in colonies of separate individuals

Compound eyes: eyes divided into many facets

Concentric: having a common centre

Condyle: ellipsoid knob-like end of a bone fitting into a socket in an adjacent bone, forming a joint allowing movement in one or two planes but no rotation

Conical: cone-shaped, tapering to a point

Coniferous: cone-bearing evergreen type of tree

Contemporaneous: living at the same time

Convergent evolution: superficial resemblance between different life-forms sharing a common mode of existence

Convoluted: folded

Coriaceous: leathery

Cornea: the outer membranous covering of the eye

Corona: the main part of the test in echinoids

Cosmine: material found in cosmoid scales

Cosmoid: scales typical of primitive chondrichthyoid fishes

Cranial: appertaining to the skull

Cranium: the skull

Crinoidal limestone: limestone deposits exhibiting many crinoid remains

Crinoids: the sea-lilies

Cryptocrystalline: a type of quartz whose crystals are not easily visible

Ctenoid: comb-like

Ctenophora: the comb-jellyfishes

Cuneiform: wedge-shaped

Cusp: the projection on the crown of a tooth

Cycloid: rounded and flattened, e.g. the scales of some fishes

Dactylozooids: the smaller zooids in hydrocorallines

Deciduous: broad-leaved tree which sheds its leaves in autumn

Dendroid: branched

Dentary: the tooth-bearing bone in the lower jaw of some fishes and amphibians

Denticles: small pointed structures found in the skin in primitive fishes

Denticulated: serrated with teeth along the edges

Dentine: the material of which the outer layer of teeth is composed

Dentition: the arrangement of the teeth in the jaws

Dermal: appertaining to the skin or external covering of the body

Dermal bones: bones situated just below the skin in the head of some fishes

Dinosaur: a collective name for giant reptiles of the Mesozoic era, more properly applied to one particular group

Diphycercal: in fishes, the tail in which both lobes are the same size

Diploblastic: composed of two layers of cells, as in coelenterates

Dipnoi: the lungfishes

Disc: the central body portion of a starfish

Discoidal: disc-shaped or depressed

Distal: the end of an appendage furthest away from the main body

Diurnal: active in the daytime

Divergence (evolutionary): producing a variety of forms within the same group adapted to widely differing types of habitat

Diverticulae: extensions from the alimentary canal

Dorsal: upper side or back

Dorsoventral: upper and lower surfaces together

Ecology: the study of the relationships between living things to their surroundings and to one another

Ectoderm: the external surface of the protoplasm

Embryo: the unborn stage of an animal

Endoderm: the inner surface of the protoplasm

Endoskeleton: skeleton inside the body

Ethmoid: the bone at the base of the nose, through perforations in which the olfactory nerves pass

Epicaudal lobe: an additional lobe to the tail in some fishes

Epitheca: a calcareous membrane covering the underside of the body in hydrocorallines

Excentric: not in the centre

Excurrent: an opening through which air, water, etc. are expelled from the body

Exoskeleton: skeleton outside the body

Femur: the upper bone of the hind limb; the thigh

Fibula: one of the lower bones of the hind limb

Fin spines: spines found on the fins of some fishes

Flagellate: equipped with a flagellum or flagella

Flagellum (pl. flagella): a whip-like extension of protoplasm facilitating movement in certain protozoans

Flexure: ability to bend, e.g. a joint

Foetus: the embryo or unborn young

Food chain: metaphorically speaking, a chain of organisms typical of a natural community, each link in the chain feeding on the nex lower one, and in turn being fed on by the next higher link. At the lowest point are always plants. Proceeding upwards, animals are larger in size but fewer in numbers.

Food grooves: grooves radiating from the mouth in cystoids and blastoids

Foramen (pl. foramina): the opening between bones through which nerves, etc. can pass

Fovea centralis: a small area in the centre of the eye governing clear perception of detail

Frond: the leaf-like structure in ferns which bears the sori or reproductive bodies

Fusiform: shuttle-shaped

Ganglion (pl. ganglia): nerve-centre in the lower animals

Ganoid: in fishes, scales composed of ganoine

Ganoine: the glossy, enamel-like substance of which many fish scales are composed

Gastrozooids: the larger zooids in hydrocorallines

Genital: appertaining to reproduction

Gills: breathing-tubes in fishes and other creatures

Ginkgo: the maidenhair tree

Gonads: reproductive glands

Gonophore: zooid-producing body

Gonotheca: the polyp producing zooids in coelenterates

Gregarious: living in groups

Gular: appertaining to the throat

Haemal arches: structures supplying blood to the gills

Herbivorous: plant-eating

Heterocercal: in fishes, the tail in which both lobes are different in size

Heterogeneous: dissimilar

Hominids: man-like forms

Homocercal: in fishes, the tail in which both lobes are alike

Homogeneous: alike

Humerus: the upper bone of the forelimb

Hydroid: the polypoid form of a coelenterate

Hydrorrhiza: the adhesive basal disc in coelenterates which fixes the body to the substrate

Hydrospires: respiratory tubes found only in blastoids

Hydrotheca: the individual polyps of a colonial coelenterate

Hyoid: the hinging bone of the jaws

Hyomandibular: jaw bone derived from what was originally the first branchial arch

Hyostylic: mode of jaw suspension in which the hyoid plays a major part

Hypocaudal: the lower lobe of the tail in fishes

Hypocercal: in fishes, the tail in which the ventral lobe is the larger

Igneous rocks: rocks formed by volcanic action

Ilium: the dorsal region of the pelvic girdle

Imbricating: overlapping, like slates on a roof

Imperforate: not perforated

Incisors: cutting teeth

Incubation: hatching period of eggs in birds, etc.

Incurrent (opening): admitting air, water, etc. into the body

Indicator fossils: fossils characteristic of a specific rock horizon

Inferior: situated lower on the body

Infra-orbital: below the eye

Infusoria: microscopic organisms found in infusions of organic substances

Insectivorous: insect-eating

Integument: exterior covering of the body

Interglacial period: period of time between two Ice Ages

Interlamina: situated between the layers

Interorbital: between the eyes

Interradial: between the rays

Interstice: a space

Interstitial: cells which fill up spaces

Intromittent: capable of being inserted

Invertebrate: animal without a backbone

Involuted: folded back on itself

Ischium: the ventral, backward-projecting part of the pelvic girdle

Isopedin: lamellated bone, as found in ganoid scales

Jaw suspension: the mode in which the jaws are attached to the skull

Keratin: the hard, horny substance found in some sponges

Lactation: the period of suckling young

Lamella: a layer. Lamellar, arranged in layers

Lamina: layer

Laminated: arranged in layers

Larva: the juvenile stage in animals which undergo metamorphosis

Lateral: situated at the side

Lateral line: in fishes, the system of sensitive pits arranged in a line
   along the sides of the body, whereby vibrations are received

Lava: molten material erupted by a volcano

Lepidotrichia: hair-fine scales in the fins of fishes

Littoral: appertaining to the seashore

Locomotor centres: the brain centres governing movement

Lumbar: the region between the ribs and the sacrum

Madreporite: the external opening of the ambulacral system in
   echinoids

Mammals: animals which suckle their young

Mammary glands: milk-producing glands in female mammals

Mandibles: jaws

Mandibular: appertaining to the jaws or mandibles

Marsupial: a pouched mammal such as the kangaroo

Matrix: the rock in which a fossil is embedded

Maxilla: one of the bones in the vertebrate upper jaw, carrying all
   the teeth except the incisors

Maxillary: a branch of the cranial nerves

Meckel's cartilage: the lower jaw in fishes

Median: situated in the middle

Median fins: the fins situated between the pectoral and pelvic fins in
   fishes

Median line: the line which can be drawn dividing a bilaterally
   symmetrical organism, or any part of the body, into right and
   left halves

Medusites: casts formed from the dead bodies of jellyfishes by the filling-in of the body cavity with mud or sand

Medusoids: the alternating generation producing the free-swimming stage in polypoid coelenterates

Membranous: composed of thin skin or membrane, e.g. wings of bats

Mesentery: vertical membranous partitions in the coelenterate body

Mesoderm: the middle layer between ectoderm and endoderm

Mesogloea: the jelly-like material separating the outer and inner layers of cells in coelenterates

Metabolism: the various processes using energy in the body

Metamorphic rocks: rocks which have undergone physical or chemical changes

Metamorphosis: change of form

Microhabitat: a habitat restricted to a smal situation, e.g. under the bark of a tree

Molars: grinding teeth

Monotremes: primitive egg-laying mammals

Morphology: the study of form

Myotemes: blocks of muscle inside the body wall in fishes, amphioxus, etc.

Nares: the nostrils

Nematoblasts: the stinging cells found in certain coelenterates

Neolithic: the second stage in man's cultural development in which stone tools were ground and polished

Neotenic: retaining the form and characteristics of the larval or juvenile stage into adult life

Neural arches: structures through which the spinal cord passes along the vertebral column

Neurocranium: the brain-case

Nocturnal: active at night

Nodule: small rounded or oval lump of rock containing a fossil

Notochord: a cartilaginous rod-like supporting structure, primitive forerunner of the vertebral column

Nuclear: appertaining to the nucleus of a cell

Obturator foramen: a process sealing off an opening in the skull

Occipital: appertaining to the forehead

Oesophagus: the tube leading to the digestive tract from the mouth

G

Olfactory: appertaining to the sense of smell
Omnivorous: eating various types of food
Operculate: possessing gill-covers
Operculum (pl. opercula): gill-cover in fishes
Ophiuroids: the brittle-stars
Orbit, orbital rim: the bony circle surrounding the eye
Orifice: any opening in the body
Ossicles: minute bone-like structures embedded in the tissues
Ossified: rendered bone-like, calcified
Osteodentine: the material of which the core of a tooth is composed
Otic: concerning the ear
Ovary: the egg-producing gonad in the female
Palaeolithic: the first stage of man's cultural development in which
    stage tools were made by chipping animal bones
Palatal: appertaining to the palate
Palatal teeth: teeth situated on the palate
Palatine: the two bones forming the hard palate
Palatoquadrate: the upper jaw in fishes
Parallel evolution: entirely unrelated animal groups acquiring
    similar characteristics in similar environments
Parasphenoid: bone adjacent to the sphenoid (q.v.)
Parietal: appertaining to the sides of the head
Pectoral: appertaining to the chest or thorax
Pectoral girdle: the bony framework to which the upper limbs are
    attached
Peduncle: stem or stalk
Pedunculate: possessing a stem or stalk
Pelagic: inhabiting the sea but not bottom-dwelling
Pelvic girdle: the bony framework to which the lower limbs are
    attached
Pentagonal: five-sided
Periphery: the outer edge
Petaloid: petal-shaped
Photosynthesis: the manufacture of starch by green plants through
    the action of sunlight on their chlorophyll
Phylum (pl. phyla): the largest group into which animals can be
    classified
Pineal foramen: the opening above the pienal gland in the
    cranium

Pinnules: the jointed processes forming the feather-like tentacles in crinoids

Placenta: a modification of the chorion attaching the embryo to the womb, whereby the embryo derives nourishment from the mother's blood-stream

Placoderms: the group of fishes characterised by aphetohyoid jaw suspension (q.v.)

Placoid scales: denticles (q.v.)

Plastron: the lower shell in tortoises and turtles

Platybasic: flat-bottomed

Poikilothermic: able to adapt body temperature to equal that of the surroundings; popularly but erroneously called 'cold-blooded'

Polygonal: many-sided

Polyp: the hydroid form of a coelenterate

Polypoid: polyp-like in form

Poriferous: pore-bearing

Predaceous: feeding on other animals

Predator: animal which feeds on other animals

Prehensile: able to cling to supporting structures

Primates: the highest mammal group, to which man and the anthropoid apes belong

Protein: a complex organic compound present in all living things and essential to life

Protoplasm: the basic substance of which living cells are composed

Protozoa: the simplest animals, consisting of only one cell

Proximal: the end of an appendage nearest to the main body

Pseudopodia: projections of protoplasm facilitating movement in amoeboid protozoans

Pterygoid: the wing-shaped bone connected with the sphenoid

Pulmonary: appertaining to the lungs

Pubis: the ventral, forward-projecting part of the pelvic girdle

Pygidium: caudal shield (q.v.)

Quadrupedal: walking on four legs

Radial: spreading outwards from the centre

Radius: one of the lower bones of the fore-limb

Rays: the 'arms' of a starfish

Relict form: a living representative of a very early ancestral type

Reticulated: covered with a network

Retina: the phototropic or light-sensitive layer of the eye

Rhizopod: an amoeboid protozoan

Rostrum: a snout-like projection or elongation of the jaws

Ruminant: animal which chews the cud

Sacrum: a group of vertebrae fused together and joined wholly or partially to the ilium

Savanna lands: tropical grasslands

Sclerenchyma: calcareous tissue in hydrocorallines

Scutes: shields

Sedimentary rocks: rocks laid down by river or ocean deposition

Selachian: shark-like

Sensory canal: the lateral line (q.v.) in fishes

Septum (pl. septa): an internal division

Serial replacement: the slow replacement of teeth in a specific succession

Sessile: attached directly to anything without a stalk

Sigmoidal: S-shaped

Siliceous: made of silica

Somite: a segment of the body

Sphenoid: the wedge-shaped bone at the base of the skull

Spheroidal: globular in shape

Spicules: small needle-shaped rods of silica, etc. found in sponges

Spiracle: the opening in front of the anterior gill-slit in chondrichthyoid fishes

Squamation: arrangement of scales

Stem reptiles: the first or original stock from which later reptile types developed

Stereoscopic vision: three-dimensional vision

Sternum: the breast-bone

Stratum (pl. strata): layer(s) of rock

Striae: superficial ridges or lines

Striated: scored with lines

Substratum: substrate, supporting layer

Superior: situated higher on the body

Supraorbital: above the eye

Suture: a line of jointing between bones or other structures

Swim-bladder: air-filled organ maintaining buoyancy in fishes

Syzygy: fusion of two adjacent stem-joints in crinoids in which the original line of division still remains visible

Tabulae: transverse calcareous partitions in hydrocorallines

Tectiform: roof-shaped

Teleosts: the advanced bony fishes

Temporal: appertaining to the forehead

Test: the hard outer shell in echinoderms

Testis: the sperm-producing gonad in the male

Tetrapods: four-footed animals

Thecodonts: a group of extinct reptiles characterised by hollow teeth set into deep sockets in the jaws

Thorax: the upper body, the chest

Tibia: One of the lower bones of the hind limb

Trachea (pl. tracheae): respiratory tubes in the lower animals

Trigeminal: one of the facial nerves

Trilobate: divided into three lobes

Tuberculate: possessing tubercles

Tubercules: rounded excrescences from the ectoderm

Ulna: one of the lower bones of the forelimb

Ungulates: hoofed animals

Unicellular: composed of only one cell

Unilocular: without septa or internal divisions

Unspiculated: without spicules

Uterus: the womb

Vascular: (tissues) containing vessels which conduct fluid

Vestigial: functions remaining only as a remnant of the original

Ventral: on the underside

Vertebrate: animal with a backbone

Viscera: internal organs

Vitreous: glassy in appearance

Vomer: the upper palate in some fishes and amphibians

Vomerine teeth: teeth attached to the vomer

Xerophytic: (plants) adapted to conserving moisture in arid conditions

Yolk: the food-supply stored in the egg for the nourishment of the embryo

Zooid: the reproductive body in coelenterates

Zoophytes: animals with certain plant-like characteristics

Bibliography

Buchsbaum, R.   *Animals without Backbones* (University of Chicago, Pelican)
Colbert, E. H.   *Men and Dinosaurs* (Evans, Pelican)
Darwin, Charles   *The Origin of Species* (Various)
Holmes, Arthur   *Principles of Physical Geology* (Nelson)
Moy-Thomas, J. A.   *Palaeozoic Fishes* (Methuen)
Rhodes, F. H. T.   *The Evolution of Life* (Pelican)
Romer, A. S.   *Man and the Vertebrates* (Pelican)
Romer, A. S.   *Vertebrate Palaeontology* (University of Chicago)
Stamp, L. Dudley   *An Introduction to Stratigraphy* (Allen and Unwin)
Swinton, W. E.   *The Corridor of Life* (Cape)
van Koenigswald, G. H. R.   *Meeting Prehistoric Man* (Thames and Hudson)

Publications of the British Museum (Natural History):
                              Evolution
                              British Cenozoic Fossils
Clark, W. E. Le Gros   *History of the Primates*
Muir-Wood, H. M., and   *The Succession of Life through Geological Time*
  Oakley, K. P.
Swinton, W. E.   *Fossil Amphibians and Reptiles*
Swinton, W. E.   *Fossil Birds*

Index

Figure numbers are shown in italics, plates in bold type

Plates

Plate 1   An Upper Devonian sponge (see pp. 33–7)
Plates 2, 3   *Receptaculites*, a fossil sponge-like form

Plate 4   *Zaphrentis prolifica*, a fossil coral (see pp. 48–51)
Plate 5   *Heliophyllum conglomeratum*, a fossil coral
Plate 6   *Lithostrotion canadensis*, a fossil coral

Plate 7   A trilobite (see pp. 52–6)
Plate 8   A phacopid trilobite associated with Silurian and Devonian rocks
Plate 9   Middle Devonian trilobites

Plate 10   An outstandingly perfect example of a crinoid

Plate 11   Crinoids (see pp. 72–6)
Plate 12   *Semionotus agassizi* (see p. 109)

Plate 13   *Undina penicillata*, a Jurassic coelacanth (see pp. 116–9)
Plate 14   Cast of the modern coelacanth *Latimeria chalumnae* Smith

Plate 15   Detail of cast of modern coelacanth

08418
5/52